*The
Extreme
Game*

# The Extreme Game

EDITED BY

## DICK WIMMER

BURFORD BOOKS

Library of Congress Cataloging-in-Publication Data
The extreme game : an extreme sports anthology / edited by Dick Wimmer.
       p.     cm.
    ISBN 1-58080-089-0
    1. Extreme sports.   I. Wimmer, Dick.
GV749.7.E98  2001
796.04—dc21                                                    2001035460

# Contents

# *Introduction*

Right off the bat, let me say I welcome all challenges to my choices and any suggestions for other extreme moments of glory.

The discussion, of course, is moot, and I offer here merely my favorites, those in certain cases less well known than others. Feel free to send along your cards and letters and e-mails, but at least open your eyes and minds to some highlight reels that you, dear, gentle reader, may have skipped by, and share these splendid achievements, as well as some extreme moments from more traditional sports. So in addition to BASE jumping and mountain climbing, ice cycling and skateboarding, I've selected Secretariat at the top of his form and A. J. Foyt in his prime, the XFL and rodeo roping, Bruce Lee and the hunting of man in "The Most Dangerous Game." Enjoy!

# *Extreeme*

## Brendan I. Koerner

*Brendan I. Koerner is a journalist who writes for* U.S. News and World Report, *where this piece first appeared.*

Kristen Ulmer is a hard-core addict, and she knows it. Ever since her first childhood schuss down a snow-covered peak, she has been hopelessly hooked on adrenaline. In her teens, she abandoned the cozy confines of ski resorts for the 70-degree inclines and 50-foot drops of rugged wilderness trails. By her early 20s, she was the nation's foremost female "radical skier," the darling of cinematographers eager to capture her perilous cliff jumps and set them to rock soundtracks for the MTV crowd.

Today, six knee operations later, Ulmer, 30, is paid by sponsors to ski down the world's tallest, remotest mountains, from Tajikistan to New Zealand. To relax, she scales towering rock formations. She has snuck into Tibet for some serious mountaineering and biked solo across India. Perversely, she says she gets a thrill from virtually any kind of risk: Hitchhiking through the desolate Alaskan interior, she was picked up by a man who threatened her life. "I got a kick out of it," she says.

Skillful, fearless—and some might say crazy—Ulmer is a leader in an athletic revolution that puts a premium on the wagering of life and limb. Adored by a young America hungry for thrills, these sports, popularly known by the Madison Avenue–created moniker "extreme sports," are popping up on urban streets, off-road trails, and television screens. Heart-racing activities such as downhill mountain biking, backcountry snowboarding, and skydiving are capturing an ever-growing chunk of the $40-billion-plus that America spends on sporting goods annually.

At the tamer end of the spectrum, in-line skating, which allows aggressive souls to zoom down steps and steep hills at over 30 miles per hour, was the fastest-growing sport of 1996 and the most popular of any sport among children and teens, according to the Sporting Goods Manufacturers Association. Rock climbing has moved from the fringe to the mainstream over the past few years; according to one estimate, a half million Americans now find joy in dangling from cliffs, up from 50,000 in 1989. Wakeboarding, a snowboarding-waterskiing hybrid that allows participants to flip, spin, and carom off buoys at high speeds, had 100,000 adherents in 1991; four years later, that figure had jumped to three-quarters of a million.

Even the most extreme of extreme sports are booming: Sky surfing, in which expert parachutists perform circus-worthy twists and turns on graphite boards while free falling from 13,000 feet, didn't exist in 1990; now it attracts thousands of devotees. And a sport known as BASE jumping (for Buildings, Antennas, Spans, and Earth), officially established in 1980, now lures hundreds, who parachute—often illegally and at night—off fixed objects such as radio towers or bridges.

This week, fans are tuning in to the weeklong X Games, the Olympics of extreme sports sponsored by cable network ESPN.

Created three years ago, the X Games have quickly evolved into a flagship franchise for the Disney-owned network. Beamed to almost 200 countries, this year's games have brought over 400 of the world's top extreme athletes to San Diego for wild thrills and epic wipeouts in prime time. Enormous crowds will line the city's streets to check out leather-clad street lugers lying supine on their souped-up skateboards, zipping along at 80 mph while hovering a mere ⁵⁄₁₆ inch off the asphalt. Spectators will clog the beach to witness snowboarders launching themselves heavenward off a 300-foot ramp covered with man-made powder. Afterward, the fans will mob extreme stars like Sergie Ventura, the recordholder for "high air" skateboarding, and wakeboarder Andrea Gaytan, a four-time world champion, and vie for autographs on their official X Games albums. Then maybe they'll run to J. C. Penney to pick up some official X Games clothing.

## Borrrring!

For those weaned on three-minute music videos and Pac-Man, the old sports standbys are simply snoozers compared with their newfangled extreme counterparts. X Games athlete T. J. Lavin, 20, who specializes in soaring high above the earth on pint-sized BMX stunt bikes, voices the attitude of many of his peers. "Baseball is so lame!" he says. "You gotta wait, like, five minutes in between pitches for something to happen. Football's the same way, just stopping and starting. But these sports are different." Ulmer concurs: "It's one thing to be a really good basketball player," she says. "But imagine if every time you missed a basket, somebody would shoot you in the head. It would be a lot more exciting, right?"

Extreme sports are not quite that dangerous. But the possibility of physical harm is very real. For most extreme athletes, busted body parts are a fact of life: In-line skating alone sent 105,000 people to the emergency room in 1995, many with fractured bones resulting from the sport's frequent body-meets-pavement collisions. Lavin, who ruptured his spleen and cracked several ribs in an accident a few years ago, says with a smile, "Man, I've bust my head open so many times I've lost count." In the more outlandish disciplines, the Grim Reaper elbows his way into the equation. Frank Gambalie, for example, an expert BASE jumper, is matter-of-fact about the risks he faces while pursuing a sport that has claimed 39 lives: "There aren't many injuries in BASE jumping. You either live or you die." Ice climbing, despite its innocuous name, also ranks particularly high on the danger list. Death is always just around the corner when you're scaling ice walls with a pair of pickaxes. Says Nancy Prichard, a prominent ice climber: "I expect to lose three to four friends a year."

Yet the threat of injury or death inherent in navigating furious rapids on a slab of Styrofoam or snowboarding down a 20,000-foot mountain fails to turn away new recruits. Quite the opposite—it is the chance of a catastrophe that makes extreme sports so enticing. A century ago, in *The Will to Believe,* the philosopher William James wrote, "It is only by risking our persons from one hour to another that we live at all." But contemporary America is a nation that seems hell-bent on expunging risk from every aspect of life. "There's always this notion in America that nobody should take risks. The toilets are clean, the hamburger meat is cooked to X degrees, there are a lot of lawyers," says Ulmer. "American culture is real scaredy-cat culture, and people are sick of it."

Michael Bane, author of *Over the Edge: A Regular Guy's Odyssey in Extreme Sports,* agrees. "The trend in society is to eliminate risk. It's gotten to the point where there are no more swings on playgrounds. At the same time, people are saying, 'Where's Indiana Jones?' People need adventure in their lives."

Frank Farley, a Temple University psychologist, believes this thirst for adventure is a fundamental aspect of the American character that refuses to wilt despite the trend toward risk elimination. Farley's research into thrill seeking has allowed him to construct a composite sketch of the typical extreme athlete, a personality model he labels "Type T—positive physical." Type T's, Farley says, tend to be extraordinarily extroverted and creative. They crave novelty and excitement. Some manifest these characteristics in the intellectual domain; Farley classifies innovative thinkers such as Albert Einstein and Francis Crick, for example, as "Type T—positive mental." Other people gravitate toward the sinister, "Type T—negative" end of the personality spectrum, abusing drugs or engaging in violent crime to indulge their appetite for thrills. Still others fit the profile of Ulmer or Lavin, satisfying their drive for excitement by participating in sports where the consequence of failure is more than just a bruised ego. "There are some people who hold on to the handrails of life—the rules, the traditions," says Farley. "The Type T's let go of the handrails. They create their own life."

America, with its roots in revolution, its prosperity grounded in the high-risk ventures of capitalism, and its mythology filled with fearless frontiersmen, is fundamentally a Type T nation—for better and for worse. Yet the circumstances of our culture have teetered toward the timid—the bland environs of suburbia, the drab rows of Dilbert-style cubicles, the numbing boredom of 28-hour-a-week TV-watching habits. Extreme sports provide a socially acceptable outlet for those Type T—positive yearnings. "George Will has said that if you want to understand America, you must understand baseball," says Farley. "No, if you want to understand America, you must know extreme sports."

## Outer Limits

Although skeptics may label extreme athletes as nuts with Freudian cravings for self-harm, Marvin Zuckerman, author of *Behavioral Expression and Biosocial Bases of Sensation Seeking,* claims that the obverse is true. "If these were real death wishers, they wouldn't bother with safety precautions," he says. "The 'death wish' is a myth made up by those who aren't high-sensation seekers, who can't understand the rewards." True to James's 19th-century pronouncement, many athletes go to the extreme because they feel most vibrantly alive when straddling the line between safety and danger. "Everybody has a kind of outer limit," says Bane, who reached his limit—and came within a hair's breadth of meeting his Maker—while "river surfing" through ferocious rapids in New Zealand. "As you approach that limit, it's almost like you kick in a certain level of problem-solving skill. You start using 18 percent of your brain instead of 16 percent." The notion that there is a life-affirming quality to big-time physical risks is an alluring one. And try as we might to deny that attraction, it often refuses to lie placidly beneath the surface. "If people go traveling to Europe and they happen to get mugged, the coolest thing they take back from that trip is that they got mugged," says Ulmer.

Type T personalities, both positive and negative, are most apt to take physical risks between the ages of 15 and 25, Farley believes, an age bracket that jibes with the youthful demographic that watches the X Games, snowboards, wakeboards, and, on the flip side, commits more than its share of violent felonies. Of course, the pricier extreme sports, such as street luging (up to $4,000 for a custom sled—leather bodysuit not included), are geared toward an older set, while pastimes that require years of practice in addition to financial resources, such as sky surfing or mountaineering, are certainly not for kids. But the guts, physical skill, and rapid healing needed to go to the extreme are most frequently found in young bodies. Journalist Bane remembers when a magazine paid him to "drop into a half-pipe"—skateboardese for entering one of the steep, U-shaped ramps where tricks are performed, and the middle-aged are usually out of place. "[My skateboarding] looked like an industrial accident," he remembers with a chuckle. "I asked a kid there what I was doing wrong. He said, 'Dude, you're thinking about the pain.' And I thought, 'Great, I'm getting Zen lessons from a 12-year-old.'"

## Do It Yourself

Extreme sports not only satisfy the need for excitement in an increasingly boring world. They also provide an outlet for the kind of creativity and individual expression often squashed in a homogenized culture of chain stores and mini malls. While baseball and football remain virtually unchanged from generation to generation, extreme athletes are constantly fiddling with the formulas to create new disciplines. A few years ago, a California skydiver named Jerry Loftis decided to try something new by jumping out of an airplane with a skateboard Velcroed to his feet. Ta-da! Sky surfing was born. In 1993, a trio of young Colorado Springs, Colorado, residents decided they wanted to enjoy the thrills of snowboarding in the summer. Presto! They invented the MountainBoard, an all-terrain skateboard-like contraption that allows snowboarders to carve turns year-round. White-water rafting begat rapid riding, in which a polystyrene float with joystick grips is used to navigate furious rivers. In-line skating begat skitching, a dangerous, city-streets favorite in which skaters launch themselves from the bumpers of speeding cars. The permutations are seemingly endless.

An upbringing in a Type T culture may not be the only factor in creating an athletic daredevil. Scientists are now beginning to investigate the possibility that chronic thrill seeking is a result of biogenetic directives. Keith Johnsgard, a professor emeritus of psychology at San Jose State University, suggests that risk seekers—a group he describes as possessing the "HSS" (high-sensation seeking) trait—may be born with a "thrill" gene that dictates their need for excitement.

A January 1996 article in the journal *Nature Genetics* gave support to this view. Scientists reported that novelty seekers—people who yearn for a constant stream of fresh, powerful stimuli—possess a gene that makes the brain especially responsive to the neurotransmitter dopamine. Working independently, teams of Israeli and American researchers found that this gene encodes instructions for the so-called D4 dopamine receptor, which Johnsgard refers to as the brain's "feel-good site." "It's the kind of site that gets hit when you take cocaine or have good sex," Johnsgard says. "Or jump out of an airplane." People who have the gene may be supersensitive to the neurotransmitter's pleasure-inducing effects and therefore especially keen on maintaining high dopamine levels. Extreme sports is one way to keep the dopamine flowing. Drug abuse is another—a recent article in the journal *Molecular Psychiatry* indicates that the same gene linked with "novelty seeking" may also predispose individuals toward heroin addiction.

Other studies have asserted that high-sensation seekers possess brains with unusually low levels of the enzyme monoamine oxidase B (MAO B), which has long been known to play a central role in regulating arousal, inhibition, and pleasure. The link between MAO B deficiency and the HSS trait is not yet entirely clear. Some researchers hypothesize that low levels of MAO B can produce sensation craving by "dampening" the impact of stimuli on the brain.

This "low arousability" spurs people to engage in highly stimulating activities—say, hurling themselves from the world's highest waterfall or surfing a 40-foot wave several miles offshore—just to reach the level of satisfaction the ordinary person might obtain from dinner and a movie.

When a high-sensation seeker gets the first taste of liberation from the "handrails of life," the experience can bring about enormous changes. Like the excitement-addicted Ulmer, some discover that they can enjoy life only when they are dedicated to the full-time pursuit of thrills. Not too long ago, Frank Gambalie spent his days in an office designing security systems—"a suit and tie and a secretary, the whole nine yards," he remembers. Flustered by the petty stresses of the cloistered 9-to-5 routine, he started bungee jumping. "I started to use bungee jumping as a drug, as a way to clean my slate," says Gambalie. "I would jump and I'd be like, 'Problems? What problems?'" Desperate for a constant adrenaline supply, he quit his job and soon became attracted to BASE jumping and its promise of a rush to surpass all rushes. He is a veteran of 456 jumps, including leaps from Yosemite's El Capitan, the San Francisco Bay Bridge, and the world's highest tram in France.

According to Johnsgard, extreme athletes like Gambalie, with their unwavering cool in the face of extraordinary circumstances, resemble the romantic heroes of spaghetti westerns or Indiana Jones–style adventures and thus pique the imaginations of those secretly wishing to put that Man With No Name swagger in their step—if not full time, then at least for a few brief moments on Saturday or Sunday. "These people are really emotionally very stable people, not moody at all," he says. "They don't suffer from a lot of fear or anxiety or depression." Johnsgard's findings are borne out by a 1991 University of Barcelona study, which found that the most daring of extreme athletes scored exceptionally low on a scale of neuroticism. The prospect of achieving a similar freedom from excessive self-consciousness is part of the appeal of extreme sports. Obsessive thoughts about slim waistlines, full hairlines, and stable bottom lines all disappear when hurtling groundward at 120 mph on a skyboard.

## Semper Fi

With their therapeutic potential vouched for by millions of John Q. Publics, extreme sports show no signs of ceasing their expansion. A sure indicator of their popularity is the way in which corporate America has scrambled to co-opt the lingo and culture of the extreme world. "I remember the Old Spice ads where the guy would walk off a ship, walk into a bar, and walk out with a great-looking blond," says Ron Semiao, the ESPN programming executive who created the X Games. "Now they show that guy in-line skating." Countless advertising slogans mimic the hypercaffeinated energy of the extreme world. X Games sponsor Pringles, the wafer-thin potato chips that come in a can, commands consumers to "Slam the Stack!"; Mountain Dew, Pepsi-Cola's nerve-jolting soda, which has carved its niche with commercials depicting gnarly dudes scampering up rocks and jumping off radio towers, screams, "Do the Dew!" Blue-chip titans like Nike and Chevrolet also have gotten into the act, signing up as X Games sponsors in order to snag young consumers. Uncle Sam is a sponsor, too, promoting his own extreme sport—the U.S. Marine Corps.

The corporate buzz may signal a shift in the athletic world, according to Temple's Farley. He predicts that extreme sports will become the major spectator and participant sports of the 21st century. "Baseball will become a minor sport," he says. "Sports that involve speed, variety, and change will replace it. Sports that are closer to the central character of this country."

Impending doom for the national pastime? This may be hard to swallow. But if the crowd gathered at an ESPN-sponsored extreme sports demonstration on a cold, damp Chicago Sunday last month is any indication, Farley may not be too far off the mark. Composed almost entirely of kids under 16, the spectators stood shivering in their extreme sports "uniforms"—baggy pants, hooded T-shirts, dyed hair, the occasional pierced lip or tongue. They "oohed!" and "aahed!" as T. J. Lavin defied gravity with his array of 360-degree spins and graceful launches into the ether. Some held skateboards or carried in-line skates slung over their shoulders, waiting for the chance to sign the obligatory release forms and try out their newest jumps on a few clumsily arranged boxes and ramps. Huge speakers blared the slogan, "If you're not living on the edge, you're taking up too much room!" And as Lavin dazzled with his tricks, crashing to earth only to rise again, one slight 11-year-old sucking on a cup of Mountain Dew spoke for the next generation of athletes. "That is so cool!" he exclaimed excitedly. "I gotta do that!"

# BASE Jumping:
# Marta Empinotti

## David Ferrell

*David Ferrell is a staff writer for the* Los Angeles Times, *from which this piece was taken.*

Usually she begins at night or dawn hopping barbed-wire fences, creeping where she can up stairwells, climbing high ladders and girders.

Her goal is elevation, the height she can reach by sneaking onto the roof of a skyscraper or the top of a radio tower. The practice is known as "stealing altitude": risking arrest to reach a precipice. For a moment she is still, and then she leaps off, free falling through space and parachuting down—a kind of Russian roulette played with shadows and distance and time.

The plunge often approaches 100 mph, creating a dose of terror far more intense than she can get by skydiving. The earth is not distant and abstract; it is right there—cars, fences, trees, all flying toward her. Her margin for error shrinks to two or three seconds. In that hyper-reality, she receives a jolt of adrenaline so intoxicating that she must have it over and over again.

"I couldn't live without it. I would die inside," Marta Empinotti says, the words streaming out in rapid Portuguese cadences. "In a way it's not a choice . . . like you don't choose to eat. I need it for my soul, to keep me balanced, to keep happy. . . . Everything is so alive when you jump. Every single hair of my body is alive."

Adrenaline junkies heavily populate the world of alternative sports; they include extreme skiers and white-water rafters, downhill mountain bikers and street luge racers, aerial surfers who dance with the clouds, and ocean surfers who skim the faces of 60-foot waves. Marta is a member of an especially hard-core breed: BASE jumpers, a narrow underground subculture as elusive as moonshiners.

BASE jumpers are the fringe of the fringe. In the 17 years since the sport was invented by four friends in a Texas living room, only 480 men and women have been awarded an official BASE number, signifying a leap from all four types of objects that constitute the acronym: Buildings, Antennas, Spans (bridges), and Earth (cliffs). That the jumps are often illegal has kept the society clandestine and elite.

Marta is BASE No. 206, a 32-year-old Brazilian with quick brown eyes and a penchant for one-liners. For more than a decade the rush has been the dominant force in her life—a singing electrical charge that has spun her halfway across the globe to high-rises in Los Angeles, Miami, and Chicago, bridges in West Virginia and northern California, cliffs in Norway, radio antennas across the South.

Three mornings a week she rises at 5 A.M. to satisfy her craving. Most of the time she jumps with friends from a 1,400-foot FM radio tower well outside this quaint college town near Daytona Beach. On nights of the full moon, she pursues the obsession to even greater extremes, driving for hours to reach a 1,250-foot antenna that affords the luxury of an elevator. Freed from the rigors of climbing, she can jump from dusk to daybreak.

Within the thinly scattered network of BASE jumpers, Marta is known worldwide, and her status is important to her. She loves the camaraderie. Most of her friends are jumpers. Her small company, Vertigo, manufactures the specialized, fast-opening rigs that BASE jumpers use. Marta spends most of her days in a narrow cinder-block room lined with sewing machines, where she works irregular hours, taking orders, stitching harnesses.

There is an easygoing charm about her. Her hair is long and honey blond, tied back in a ponytail. She wears faded jeans or combat fatigues. Her eyes crinkle with laughter as she tells stories about her jumps: the day she went topless and her canopy malfunctioned. "We call it the 'topless malfunction.'"

Being a Sagittarius, she says, she enjoys the outdoors at odd hours: the foggy dawns when the landing area is blanketed in white. The dewdrops bejeweling the spiderwebs. The nights when the sky is a glittery black slate.

Although Marta admits that the subterfuge of the sport can be exciting—her eyes light up as she recalls a night she was chased by a police helicopter—she has been busted three times. The fine for jumping cliffs at Zion National Park was more than $1,000. She would love the chance to leap from the 1,454-foot Sears Tower in Chicago—so far an unconquered object—or the 1,483-foot Petronas Towers in Kuala Lumpur, Malaysia, the world's tallest buildings, but the chances of going to jail, or being roughed up by foreign police, are just too daunting. "It's not worth it," she says. "I'm just having fun. Now you're going to put me in jail, mistreat me? I'm not a terrorist. I'm not used to roughness with people being impolite."

She is gracious, sensitive, but also a woman of contradictions. Her breeziness masks an acute mind that knows the velocity of a falling body at any designated second and the heights of buildings, antennas, and bridges all over the nation.

She loves her sport, though close friends have died doing it. She shrugs and downplays the dangers—"We know we're going to live"—but before every BASE jumping trip she phones her parents in Porto Alegre, Brazil, in case final words from her might be a comfort.

She climbs antenna girders at 1,000 feet, despite recurring bouts of dizziness. Years ago she passed out during a climb; two other jumpers had to pin her to a ladder several hundred feet up, supporting her weight until she regained consciousness.

Harsh sun wakens her. Every two hours she must eat. Requiring eight hours of sleep, she is often too busy working, traveling, and jumping, and settles for six or seven.

Marta talks about slowing down—"just a little bit"—but has difficulty doing that. Not feeling quite right, she will afix a carabiner—a metal ring—to her vest and create a tether to secure herself while climbing, rather than miss the action.

If she started out with nine lives, surely she has expended a few. How many might she have left?

Marta laughs. "I owe a couple."

Rising in the Florida dusk, the 1,250-foot antenna is a ladder to the stars: a skinny, three-sided spike of crisscrossing girders nearly as tall as the Empire State Building. Steel guy wires hold it upright: at various elevations strobe lights flash a warning to aircraft—a slow arterial pulse.

Marta and her friends roll along a weedy dirt road and hide their van deep in a tangle of shrubs and trees. With her are Mario Richard, 31, who came down from Quebec to find and jump this tower, and Kiddi Palsson, 30, a jumper from Iceland.

Like a guerrilla soldier, white-haired Bob Neely emerges from the shrubs to greet them. By far the oldest, at 48, he is a local who often jumps here alone, gaining access through the antenna's protective fence by knowing the combination to the padlock. An affable, cocksure professional skydiver, he made his first BASE jump in Louisiana from a 1,800-foot microwave tower, one of the most perilous types of antennas. On a microwave tower, your dental fillings may heat up like kernels of popcorn.

Radio engineers warn against climbing on any type of TV or radio antenna. An AM tower is so charged from top to bottom with electrical current that it can sear the flesh if you touch it while standing on the ground. Even an FM antenna like this one packs a heavy punch of non-ionizing radiation whose health effects are uncertain—thus a posted sign: CAUTION! HIGH LEVEL RADIO FREQUENCY ENERGY AREA. KEEP OUT.

Marta passes the sign without a glance, wearing military-style camouflage pants she has owned 11 years. Arc lights affixed to a low equipment building throw harsh shadows across her face. The setting is surreal: boxy machinery of indistinguishable purpose thrashing and booming like an old washing machine, hundreds of spiders overrunning the steep metal stairs and high catwalk that lead to the base of the tower. The tower itself, perhaps a dozen feet in diameter, is unimaginably tall and forbidding, nothing but forged steel.

The elevator is a perforated metal box no larger than a phone booth. The contraption is slow—12 minutes one-way—so everyone will ride at once: Marta and Bob inside, Mario and Kiddi on the roof, up in the cables and passing girders. A jarring metal screech and it begins to climb, the ground receding outside the collapsible metal door.

At 500 or 600 feet up, something goes wrong—the overloaded elevator starts slipping: rising a few feet, dropping back, rising, slowing, dropping. The lurching progress is accompanied by grating and grinding noises, bringing a dark look to Marta's face.

"Bob, shouldn't we stop?"

He shakes his head. "As long as it's going. . . ."

The elevator continues to lurch, speeding up, slipping, rising again. They fret over the likelihood of a free fall, or the motor burning out. Near 700 feet Marta suggests that maybe they should stop and get out and climb. Bob watches the girders moving by. "Come oonnnn, little choo-choo."

Jean and Carl Boenish, two skydiving photographers from Hawthorne, were half of the foursome who sat in Phil Mayfield's liv-

17

ing room in Houston in the fall of 1980 and devised a name for their sport. Jean, BASE No. 3, a dark-haired, bespectacled woman who admits she looks like a librarian, still maintains The Book—the blue three-ring ledger that records the sport's milestones. Its pages are filled with the names of all 480 jumpers who have completed the BASE jumping cycle, as well as the 39 who have died in accidents. Jean's husband Carl, BASE No. 4, appears in both columns: He was killed jumping a cliff in Norway in 1984.

Long before the sport was given a name, people were parachuting from tall objects. Someone had leaped from the Statue of Liberty around 1920. Yosemite's El Capitan had been jumped from a number of times in the 1960s and 1970s. New York's World Trade Center had been leaped from in 1975.

What the founders did was create a framework for an underground society that was waiting to emerge. Phil Smith, BASE No. 1, planned the first jumps from radio antennas. He devoted weeks to spying on security guards and doing trials with weights and parachutes. Phil liked to experiment, conceiving challenges befitting a high school physics book; in 1983, he hurled himself from a train as it rolled across a 300-foot-high bridge above the Pecoe River.

"We had to figure out how fast we were going on the bridge, how far we had to jump to clear the bridge, and where to exit to clear the rocks down below," Phil says. Now 45, with two teen daughters and retired from BASE jumping, he is proud of having been a pioneer. "There wasn't reference material. There wasn't someone to call."

Slowly the network fanned out, a loose, far-flung affiliation of daredevils and mavericks. Marta's friends are scattered to Hell and back—Hell being the name of a small town in the Cayman Islands where Lee Marcoux claims to be the only BASE jumper in the West Indies. One of Marta's favorite jumping partners is John Vincent, 29, of New Orleans, the fourth and most recent person to have leaped from the World Trade Center. That stunt, in 1991, was followed a year later by an even more audacious feat: John, wearing suction cups, scaled the 630-foot face of the St. Louis arch, a two-hour climb that ended in a short, breathtaking leap, several moments of TV airtime, and three months in federal prison.

Such spectacles have created tension within the world of BASE jumping. In another well-known incident, years ago, John was caught leaping during the day from an unfinished high-rise in Atlanta, a blunder that ruined the object for the local jumpers. They were so infuriated they tracked him down in New Orleans; three men burst into his room, bound his wrists and ankles in duct tape, and administered that age-old ignominy: a tarring and feathering.

Times change—the principal assailant is now one of John's best friends—but John is again at odds with the purists, joining a faction of BASE jumpers intent on making legal jumps for financial gain. He has appeared in TV commercials and magazine ads. He and Marta were scheduled to perform this year at the Super Bowl in New Orleans, until a bungee jumper was killed during rehearsals for a different act and their gig was canceled.

By obtaining permits and working with local authorities, BASE jumpers have organized a growing number of legal competitions. West Virginia is the site of one of the oldest: "Bridge Day," the third Saturday in October, the one day of the year that jumps are allowed from the new River Gorge Bridge. Hundreds leap from the 876-foot-high span and land in the river rapids or on the rocky shoreline.

The attention appalls many purists. They fear more publicity will mean more jumpers and more security at prime objects that will never be legal no matter what. Silence and chicanery are the only way to protect their domain, they believe.

Jumpers have been known to finagle keys, to pick locks, to scam their way past lobby guards by wearing sports jackets and ties, carrying their parachute rigs in gift-wrapped boxes. Often they perch on rooftops like gargoyles, waiting hours for nightfall so they can take wing. As with illicit sex, the secrecy heightens the thrill, at least for some. "It brings out the James Bond in you," as one jumper put it. "It has to stay hush-hush."

Word of exceptional jumping spots filters through the network. Buildings under construction are often ideal; usually they have stairwells but no windows, multiple points of entry, and minimal security. A new high-rise going up in, say, San Francisco, is likely to come to Marta's attention in Florida.

Although she may or may not travel there, her circle of friends offers entrée where she chooses. Local knowledge is important, especially around buildings, where landing areas are notoriously small and winds can play havoc. Even aside from the sport's illegalities, many professional skydivers refuse to attempt a BASE jump because it is so much more dangerous.

"I would say it's 10 times as risky," says James Hayhurt, 44, a board member of the United States Parachuting Association and a veteran of more than 4,000 skydives. "I personally would never do it. I always open [the parachute] at 2,500 feet; that gives me 15 seconds of time to deal with an emergency."

The parachuting group's guidelines say a skydiver can be barred from drop zones if he opens below 2,000 feet. In BASE jumping, there are no rules; canopies pop between 1,000 and 200 feet, sometimes even lower. If this suggests that jumpers have a death wish, most deny it. "I've got 9,000 skydives," one jumper says. "If I had a death wish, I would have failed one of them."

Still, the need for an adrenaline hit causes some jumpers to keep raising the stakes, balancing their own skills and past successes against the perceived likelihood of death. Mike Muscat, 45, of Van Nuys nearly killed himself trying to earn his BASE number in Oakland, jumping at night from a 30-story building. His chute malfunctioned, opening in a direction that carried him straight backward. He sailed through an open window and crash-landed, breaking his ankle and lying semiconscious for hours before being discovered by a construction crew.

Bill Legg, best known for unscrewing window mounts and leaping from the top of Houston's 570-foot San Jacinto Monument in 1989, figures he's broken 30 bones during his 42 years on earth. To heighten his own flow of adrenaline, he ignores the advice of friends who urge him to wear a reserve chute.

At Bridge Day in 1987, Bill stood at the river's edge and watched two accidents in a row. The first was relatively minor: Phil Smith's lines became twisted, plunging him into a boulder that shattered his left foot and right kneecap.

Medics were loading him into an ambulance when a blond, Nordic-looking jumper named Steve Gyrsting, only 25, pulled the cord on a chute that failed to deploy, then yanked on a reserve that was too slow to open. He smashed into the river at more than 100 mph.

"You could tell he was fixin' to die," Bill remembers.

Marta was watching the same jump from up on the bridge. Steve was her boyfriend. They had been going together for two years.

From the exit point, 1,150 feet up the antenna, the flat Florida landscape stretches in all directions—mowed fields, dark clumps of trees, an inky depression that gives this object its nickname, the "Black Hole." A stiff breeze shoves broken clouds across the moon.

The balky elevator has delivered the jumpers to a tiny platform contained within the tower. From there they will climb through the girders—any false step could mean a fall of several hundred feet—and fling themselves out into the night.

The direction of the breeze is critical. Mario sets adrift a scrap of tissue paper. It disappears into the darkness between the guy wires, a good sign; when the wind blows it directly toward the wires, the risk of the chutes getting caught there is too great to leap. Conditions now are ideal save for one last-minute problem: a single headlight suddenly visible far below, a one-eyed car creeping along a farm road. The jumpers must wait. Ten minutes go by before the car disappears and they edge into position, gloved hands gripping the tower.

Bob leaps first, then Marta. Fit and sinewy, she moves with sureness; the years have made her comfortable on a tower. Her hiking boots find balance on a girder and she springs out, her body disappearing into the blackness.

At 400 feet, a metal deck encircles the tower. This is the point where Marta pulls, dropping at nearly 100 mph after a six-second free fall. The canopy emerges with a sound like a crumpling paper cup, black and rectangular, a set of raven wings invisible against the sky. Gliding in long arcs, she swings below the moon and the guy wires before landing in the grass.

The jumpers stumble forward as they hit, grinning and laughing. Marta gives Kiddi a high-five as he swoops to the ground near her. The rigs are carried back to the tower and repacked under the arc lights.

The gear Marta manufactures—considered among the best in the sport—is reinforced to withstand the jolt of quick openings. The speed with which they deploy is regulated by the size of the pilot chute—a small round one that emerges first, dragging the larger canopy into the air—and by a mesh device called a "slider" that controls the separation of the chute lines. The canopies themselves are larger than those used in skydiving and are designed for a slower forward movement.

Repacking, the jumpers discuss the one-eyed car. Marta recalls a night when a tower worker showed up unexpectedly, forcing them to shut down the elevator and run. They left, grabbed a bite, and came back, lurking out of sight until the worker finally left at 1:30 A.M., when they reclaimed the antenna.

"And this other jumper goes, 'We're like cockroaches,'" Marta says, her laugher filling the night. "That's exactly how I felt, because as soon as he turned his back, man, we were in, and we jumped until sunrise."

The sky became her escape. This was long ago, a young woman eager to see the world, a young man wanting her to stay and get married. Marta was just 20, one of four sisters from an upper-class family in Porto Alegre, contemplating a career as a psychiatrist. Her wanderings—to Europe, the United States—led to a split.

"He got tired of me always taking off, so he broke up with me," she recalls. "I was very devastated. . . . And a friend of mine called me and said, 'Guess what I did this weekend—I went sky-diving.'"

She wanted to try it. Loved it. Putting off medical school for one long, last tour of the world, she ended up settling in Florida. At a drop zone there she met Steve, a tall, outgoing mechanical engineer who built jet engines. On weekends they jumped from planes. Steve admired her joyous spirit; he'd tell her, "I hope life is always pink for you."

It was Marta's idea to attempt a BASE jump—Bridge Day, October 1986. There were 15 mph winds, and Steve tried to discourage her. She did it anyway, deploying her chute so late that the jolt made her see stars. Two months later, she made her first jumping trip, a two-week sojourn to Los Angeles, forming quick friendships with those in the underground. She was hooked. Steve finally tried a jump in early 1987. That October, at Bridge Day, he died.

"I had this distorted idea that . . . life was very pretty. If you worked hard, you could get what you wanted. *Bang,* he disappeared, and every breath I took I was further away from him. When that happened, it hit me: It's not like that. You can get a lot of things, but certain things you just can't."

She couldn't jump for six months. She would climb a tower, look down, and cry. Marta was confused, aching, almost ready to give up the sport. She finally made her return by jumping the 760-foot Auburn Bridge near Sacramento. In a bad frame of mind, she planned a three-second free fall and instead took five.

"I didn't want to let go of my pilot chute. I shouldn't have been jumping. It was like a fight with myself. I wanted to die. I wanted to be with Steve."

Landing safely on the rocky river shore, she endured a reprimand from a friend. The enthusiasm began to return soon afterward during the frenzied nocturnal "campaigns" of L.A., when hundreds of covert jumps were carried out from the unfinished skeletons of office towers on Bunker Hill. She was drawn to a man from Redondo Beach named Mark Hewitt, BASE No. 46, a pioneer she much admired. Mark, Marta found out, was "naked BASE No. 1," the first to jump all four types of objects in the nude. "And I go, 'Who is naked BASE No. 2?'" Nobody, she was told. She couldn't believe it. "It's the coolest number. I'm not into numbers, but this number, this is a cool one. And I go, 'I want to be naked BASE No. 2.'"

She accomplished that mission, wearing only a helmet, kneepads, shoes, and her parachute, looking "like a character in a Monty Python movie." Naked BASE Nos. 1 and 2 were married in 1989, a turbulent union that lasted four years. Jumping was what held them together. "Whenever we had problems," Marta says, "we would plan a BASE jumping trip."

Mark ended up in Hawaii, a professional skydiver with 720 BASE jumps now. Marta kept Vertigo, the firm they launched together. A modest operation—there are only two employees—it is the primary source of her income. Looking ahead, she has begun to study for her pilot's license, hoping someday to fly commercial aircraft.

Over a beer she can talk for hours about jumps that fill her logbook: her lines getting twisted in a leap off Half Dome, crashing into a narrow ledge that saved her. Seeing herself plunge down the side of a mirrored office building in Caracas, Venezuela, in a jump for a Ruffles potato chip commercial. Landing in the trees below 3,200-foot Angel Falls in Venezuela. Being hit by lightning in South Africa, just enough to cause a day of soreness. Cliff jumping at dawn, the suspended rock climbers winking their flashlights at her, like so many wonderful fireflies.

"It's a good life. I like my life a lot," Marta says, beaming. Had she gone down a different road, become that psychiatrist she once planned to be, she would assess herself this way: "I think I'm more balanced than most people. I think I'm fortunate to know what my inner being and soul really loves."

No regrets, no guilt—not even over Steve's death. "It's still very sad for me," she says. "I'll never get over it in a way. But I never feel guilty. Even when I take a student jumping, I always make sure the person knows the risks. Steve made his own decision."

Her canopy, packed for a leap from 800 feet, opens too quickly for her when she jumps again from 1,150. Marta walks away with an aching neck. But by now it is time to rest for a while, and she naps in a sleeping bag in the high weeds. Mario and Kiddi lie in the van, Bob on the unprotected outdoor deck of the antenna, 400 feet up. "No mosquitoes," he explains, "and you always wake up a half hour before dawn." Just don't roll off the bed.

At dawn there is time for one last trip up the elevator. It will be a special jump—No. 500 for Marta and Bob both, a milestone they have decided to reach together. High over Florida, the two friends kiss, and then all four jumpers edge out onto the girders. In unison they leap, a rare four-way, the chutes popping open one by one on the way down. In the field they laugh, taking snapshots, relishing the glory of the rising Florida sun.

"That was primo!" Marta exults. By the look on her face, life has never been more pink.

# *George Mallory of Everest*

## Conrad Anker and David Roberts

*Conrad Anker is a professional mountaineer who has made breakthrough first ascents from the Himalayas to Antarctica and Patagonia. David Roberts, a mountaineer with extensive Alaskan experience, is the author of* In Search of the Old Ones *and* A Newer World. *This selection is taken from their book,* The Lost Explorer.

Sometime on the morning of June 8, 1924, George Mallory and Sandy Irvine set out from Camp VI, at 26,800 feet on the northeast ridge. The day before, the porters who had carried gear and food up to the camp in support of the summit bid brought down a note from Mallory, addressed to the expedition cinematographer, John Noel, who was ensconced at Camp III, more than 5,000 feet below.

Dear Noel,

We'll probably start early tomorrow (8th) in order to have clear weather. It won't be too early to start looking for us either crossing the rock band under the pyramid or going up skyline at 8.0 P.M.

Yours ever,
G. Mallory

Noel had a 600-millimeter lens that the expedition members used like a telescope to track their teammates' movements high on Everest. All subsequent commentators have assumed, as Odell did on reading the note, that Mallory's "8.0 P.M." was a slip of the pen, that he meant to write "8 A.M." In that case, Mallory's estimate of where he would be was exceedingly optimistic, for it was rare in the era of early Himalayan campaigns for a pair of climbers to get off from any high camp before 6:30 in the morning.

The 1924 expedition was the third of three attempts—all British—on the world's highest mountain; it followed a thorough-going reconnaissance in 1921 and a nervy assault the year after. Only Mallory had been a member of all three expeditions. Yet the weather in May 1924 had proved atrocious, defeating a very strong team's efforts even to put themselves in position for the summit thrust. Later the tea planters in Darjeeling would aver that for at least the previous 20 years, " no such weather had been known at this season."

Then, with the climbers' hopes all but extinguished, the mountain had laid a spell of grace upon them, giving them day after day of fine weather, although the men woke each morning dreading the onset of the inevitable monsoon, which, normally arriving around June 1, would enfold the Himalaya in a four-month miasma of heavy snow.

As Mallory and Irvine closed their canvas tent and headed along the windswept ridge, they were full of bursting anticipation. Only four days before, their teammate E. F. "Teddy" Norton, at the end of the gallant effort, had reached 28,126 feet—the highest anyone had ever climbed—before turning back a mere 900 feet below the summit. Norton had made his gutsy push without the aid of bottled oxygen. Mallory and Irvine were breathing gas, and though Mallory had initially been a skeptic about its efficacy, on the 1922 expedition he had learned firsthand that climbers aided by oxygen high on Everest could easily double the climbing speed of those without.

On the 1924 assault, as he had during the two previous expeditions, Mallory had proven himself the strongest and most ambitious climber. By now, his personal obsession with Everest had cranked as tight as it could be wound. In a letter to his wife, Ruth, written six weeks before from Chiblung, on the approach to Everest, he had predicted, "It is almost unthinkable . . . that I shan't get to the top; I can't see myself coming down defeated."

If his 22-year-old companion was daunted by Mallory's hubris, he gave no indication of it. In his diary only four days before his own attempt, awaiting the outcome of Teddy Norton's bold summit bid with teammate Howard Sommervell, Irvine had written, "I hope they've got to the top, but by God, I'd like to have a whack at it myself."

Ever since 1924, observers have wondered why Mallory chose Irvine as his partner for the second summit attempt, rather than the far more experienced Noel Odell, who had rounded into incomparable form at high altitude during the preceding week. Irvine had very little climbing experience, with only an exploratory outing in Spitsbergen under his belt. (In a letter to Ruth, Mallory had voiced a qualm, "wish Irvine had a season in the Alps.") But on Everest, the Oxford undergraduate had proved to be tougher than several of his more seasoned comrades, an uncomplaining worker, and a delightful companion. He was also something of a mechanical genius, who had taken apart the oxygen apparatus in the field and rebuilt it in a lighter and more efficient form. And since oxygen would be the key to Mallory's all-out dash for the summit, it made sense to have Irvine along.

That day, June 8, 1924, among the rest of the team, only Odell, climbing solo up to Camp VI in support of the summit duo, was high on the mountain. A professional geologist, he had chosen the day to wander in zigzags up the north face, looking for unusual formations. By late morning, he was swimming in a private ecstasy, for there, in one of the most barren places on earth, he had discovered the first fossil ever found on Everest.

At 12:50 in the afternoon, Odell mounted a small crag around 26,000 feet just as the clouds abruptly cleared. Squinting upward, he was treated to the brief vision that has beguiled and tantalized all Everest students since. As Odell later wrote:

> I saw the whole summit ridge and final peak of Everest unveiled. I noticed far away on a snow slope leading up to what seemed to me to be the last step but one from the base of the final pyramid, a tiny object moving and approaching the rock step. . . . I could see that they were moving expeditiously as if endeavouring to make up for lost time.

Then the clouds closed over the scene. Odell climbed on to Camp VI, where he found, to his mild alarm, pieces of oxygen equipment strewn about the tent, suggesting that Irvine had perhaps made some desperate last-minute adjustment to the apparatus. And Odell was disturbed that he had seen his pair of friends still well below the summit pyramid at almost 1 P.M., or five hours after Mallory's blithe prediction. An afternoon snow squall cleared, but now Odell could see no signs of human presence on the upper ridge, bathed in warm sunlight. He scrambled some 200 feet above the camp, whistling and yodeling in case Mallory and Irvine should be nearing it on their descent. Then, with a heavy heart, Odell headed down the mountain, as Mallory had ordered him to, for the small tent at Camp VI could not hold three climbers.

During the next two days, in an astonishing performance, Odell climbed first to Camp V, then alone all the way back up to Camp VI. When he found the tent exactly as he had left it on June 8, he knew the worst. He laid two sleeping bags in the snow in a figure T—the preaaranged signal to a teammate watching below that all hope was lost.

On May 1, 1999, Conrad Anker, one of the world's strongest mountaineers, discovered Mallory's body lying facedown, frozen into the scree and naturally mummified at 27,000 feet on Everest's north face. The condition of the body, as well as the artifacts found with Mallory, including goggles, an altimeter, and a carefully wrapped bundle of personal letters, are important clues in determining his fate. Seventeen days later, Anker free climbed the Second Step, a 90-foot sheer cliff that is the single hardest obstacle on the north ridge. The first expedition known to have conquered the Second Step, a Chinese team in 1975, had tied a ladder to the cliff, leaving unanswered the question of whether Mallory could have climbed it in 1924. Anker's climb was the first test since Mallory's of the cliff's true difficulty. In treacherous conditions, Anker led teammate Dave Hahn from the Second Step to the summit.

*Sitting beside Mallory on May 1, I looked east toward the descent route he and Irvine would have taken had they summited that June 8. I imagined Mallory's awareness even in extremis: no radio to communicate with others, no chain of fixed ropes to guide him down the mountain, no teams of rested climbers ready to enact a rescue, no way of telling the world what really happened.*

*I can only guess what Mallory's and Irvine's last moments were like, but what I do know is how their achievement has affected our climbing legacy. The boldness of their last climb formed a stepping-stone to the future. The debate over oxygen and its ultimate acceptance made it possible for their successors—including Hillary and Tenzing—to visit high places with a reasonable safety margin.*

*Sometimes late at night, I wonder whether by discovering Mallory I've aided in the destruction of a mystery. The possibility haunts me. Has my find somehow taken some of the enigmatic glory away from the 1924 expedition?*

*Others may think so, yet for me, the discovery only increases my admiration for these pioneer climbers, whose story—which will never be told in its entirety—has always lain wrapped in the secrets of Chomolungma, Mother Goddess of the Snows. I feel privileged to have participated in casting new light onto this mystery. Ultimately, Mallory and Irvine's greatest achievement was an inspirational one, for even in failure, their magnificent attempt showed us what the human spirit is capable of.*

# The Last Step: The American Ascent of K2

## Rick Ridgeway

*Rick Ridgeway is a world-class mountaineer, filmmaker, and writer. His latest book is* Below Another Sky. *This excerpt is taken from* The Last Step: The American Ascent of K2.

*Everything was ready. Now study it, Ridgeway; think. Imagine what my IQ score would be right now. Even a half-wit chimpanzee could do better than this. John's probably halfway up the snow gully by now, on his way to the summit snowfield. How long have I been fiddling with this contraption? Five minutes? Twenty minutes? This is like being loaded on dope. Can't think right. Don't even know how much time has passed. Too bad my watch broke. Don't let my mind wander; focus on this problem. O.K. It's simple: It worked before, when I tested it in the tent, so therefore it has to work now. Try putting the strap through the other loop, around the nosepiece on the mask, then back through the bottom loop. That doesn't look right, either. John must be halfway to the top by now. If I don't hurry, I'll never make it. He climbs faster than I do anyway. Maybe I'll just end up staying here all day, fiddling with this mask, while he climbs to the summit. The thought of that chimpanzee comes to mind again. Remember a picture I once saw of a chimp wearing eyeglasses, sitting and staring con-*

*foundedly at a book. The same thought now, only it's me, Rick Ridgeway, sitting just like the chimp, staring confoundedly at my oxygen mask. O.K., now don't let my mind wander; focus on this mask. Let's see, what else can I do?*

*Try to climb K2 without oxygen?*

*Can I do it?*

I had been performing satisfactorily up to that point, without oxygen, carrying the dead weight of the cylinder. Without that hindrance it would be even easier. But there were over a thousand feet to go. What would it be like a twenty-eight thousand? Would it be possible for me? I considered the danger of pulmonary edema. If that happened, there would be no hope. My lungs would fill with blood, and I would die.

I had to make some decision fast. I was quickly losing body temperature, starting to shiver. I needed to move to regain warmth. The wind was still dropping, but even the direct sun failed to warm. I looked again at my regulator, and the chance that I could correctly adjust the straps seemed remote.

What about brain damage? I knew there was that risk; it was a real concern. Brain cells do not replace themselves; cerebral damage from hypoxia is a clinical fact. I had another whimsical thought: If I had any brains to begin with, I wouldn't be up here at over twenty-seven thousand feet on K2 freezing to death, so what have I got to lose?

I chuckled at the thought.

I realized I was getting dingy.

I was very, very cold.

I set the mask and regulator in the snow, removed the bottle from the pack. Putting on the near-empty pack, I grabbed my ax and started across the traverse. I would climb without oxygen, and I would put every ounce of energy remaining in my body into reaching the summit. I thought, *I might just be able to make it.*

## September 7. Summit Pyramid, About 28,000 Feet, 2:30 P.M.

*There are only two hundred more feet at the most even though I'm not sure I can lift my foot and then the next foot and the next until I get to the top. Not after coming this far. Not this close.*

*So up goes my boot and crampon. There, that's better, now breathe a few times, and think about that next step. This will be over soon, and the sooner I lift the next foot, the sooner it will be over. Keep thinking: I've come this far, I have to make it.*

*I can't lift the foot. I can't move up any higher. Have to rest, have to rest, have to rest.*

*No. I cannot.*

*John is ahead of me. Look up at him. See, he's still moving, and moving faster than me. He has been breaking most of the trail. I can't let him do all the work. I have to do my share. So lift my foot and catch up and help break trail. There. That's better. Now think about the next foot.*

*When will it end?*

*John is stopping to rest. He is hunkering over his ax, head down, facing the slope. I must catch him. If I can make ten more steps I can reach him, and then rest, but not before. That is it: Ten steps, then rest. O.K., now up with the foot, breathe, breathe, breathe, and another stop. No good, can't make it. Have to stop for a minute, getting dizzy again. John is still resting. Only four or five steps and I can rest too. Lift a foot. Now only three more steps, now one more step and I can rest. Careful, don't collapse, don't slide down the slope. Rest on my ax.*

"You O.K.?"

"Slow. Hard to breathe. Forcing each step. Sorry I'm not breaking more trail."

"Can you lead a little?"

"I'll try. Need to rest first."

"We're close—maybe a hundred fifty feet."

"If that is the summit. If not, if it is farther behind the ridge, don't know if I can make it . . ."

"Don't worry, we've got it now."

*John is right. We have it now, keep remembering that. We are too close not to make it.*

*I must get up; I must move on. This will soon be over. No more getting up at 3 A.M., no more freezing in predawn starts. I can sit in a hot bath and feel the steaming water on my skin. Never again for the rest of my life will I take a bath and not think of this moment I wanted to soak in steaming water, so get going and soon I can have that bath.*

*Lift a foot.*

*Carefully place my crampons. This surface is irregular, small crescent patterns in the ice, and my ankles hurt from twisting to the angle of the slope.*

*Lift a foot.*

*Noise and voices. Like there are many people around me, like on a crowded train with everyone talking. Echoes, noises, voices. A din like a million voices. But that's crazy, there is no one around.*

*Lift a foot.*

*Fingers are so hard. There is no doubt this time they are frozen. It's strange, like my fingers are made of a foreign material. Must be what artificial limbs are like. It's my right hand, mostly, because that is the hand I've been holding my ax in. I should switch hands. But then my left hand would freeze, and since my right is already frozen, why freeze my left too. Does that make sense? I guess so, keep the ax in my right hand.*

*Lift a foot.*

*Look at the slope, scimitar-shaped, arching upward brilliant white against purple sky. The left side of the summit slope drops away, and I can see a steep rock ridge joining the summit slope near the top. Is that the finish to Bonington's route? It would be too hard to climb that the way I feel now. Could anyone do it? Maybe a future generation of climbers? Poor Nick Estcourt, down there somewhere buried in ice.*

*Lift a foot.*

*How nice it would be to sit on a warm beach. A tropical beach with white sand and palm trees. It's easy to imagine, look there, in front of me, I can even see a palm tree now, in the sand, growing there, in the snow. Lift a foot.*

*John is just behind me. I've been leading now for some time, but I've only come, what?—twenty feet since I rested. It seems so far, though. There is a slightly offset edge in the ice surface—a convenient mark—about another twenty feet in front. Focus on it. Begin stepping until I get there. Think of nothing else.*

*Lift a foot.*

*Breathe, breathe, breathe, gasp hard, even then I can't get enough air.*

*Lift a foot, another, another, keep going to the mark.*

*It's close. Keep going.*

*Getting dizzy, head pounding, noises—the voices, the voices. Keep going, force it out from somewhere, somehow force out the will to step, to lift the foot, the mark is close, one more step.*

*I made it.*

*Breathe, breathe, breathe. Getting dizzy again, spinning, can't get enough air. Can't breathe fast enough. Don't panic, keep control, breathe fast. Feel like I'm drowning, will my lungs explode?—don't panic. Lean on my ax. Breathe fast. There, the dizziness is starting to go away, but the voices, the voices.*

"You O.K.?"

"Have to rest. Tried to go too fast. Hallucinating."

"I'll take the lead."

*Rest while John climbs. He is stronger than I am. How can he do it? He is doing most of the step-kicking. I can't do my share. Not enough strength. But we are close now. Maybe fifty feet to the summit ridge. Hope to God the summit is close behind the ridge. If it's farther . . .*

*Get up, follow John. It's so much easier following in his steps. Sections of the ice are hard and it doesn't matter who leads, but sometimes the crust breaks, and that is when John's job is hardest.*

*Lift a foot.*

*It's not bad the first few steps after I've rested. But then each one starts getting harder. My body is screaming for oxygen. Each step harder, need to breathe more. The farther away from the last rest, the harder, but I can't rest again. Not now.*

*Lift a foot.*

*So close. Soon it will be over. John is maybe fifteen feet ahead, now maybe twenty. He is climbing faster. He is making the last steps to the summit ridge. His head is even with the ridge, now he is on it.*

*What does he see? How far is the summit? He isn't saying anything. Is it farther behind? Do we still have more to go? How can I do it?*

*Lift a foot.*

*Catch up to John. He is resting on the top of the ridge. Close now, only a few more feet. He isn't saying anything. But I can't talk to him because I have to breathe fast.*

*Stop. He is ten feet away. Look at him. He is looking down at me. Breathe a few times so I can talk.*

"Can you see it? How far? How far to the top?

John is looking at me. Now he is smiling. Is it good news?

"Fifty feet. A fifty-foot walk up a gentle slope and we're on the summit."

## September 7. The Summit of K2, 28,250 Feet, 3:30 P.M.

No wind. No clouds. Cerulean sky, brilliant sun, and at once a feeling of warmth through the thick parka, and also a strange cold. Nothing quite real, the feeling of dream. Below, a world falling in all directions. Snow peaks too numerous to identify, and glaciers traveling to distant horizon. Quiet, but an inner noise, a ringing in the ear. A thought: As an old man I will often recall this moment; I must try to remember it. It must be important. But there is failure to feel much emotion. The only feeling is absolute fatigue.

We were on the summit. We had made the last few steps together, arm in arm. From the summit ridge it was an easy walk to the highest point, but just short of it John had stopped.

"It may be corniced. Summits usually are. I'm not going up there."

He spoke with much finality. Neither of us seemed to remember Lou and Wick had been there the day before and had reported no cornice. But we were beyond remembering, beyond rational thinking, operating only on instinct. I thought, *It may be corniced, but we've come too far not to reach the very pinnacle.*

I volunteered to belly-crawl up to the highest point. John stood back, holding my ankles. I eased up to the edge, and peered over. There was solid snow under me, and the south face dropped down so steeply, about twelve thousand feet, I had a euphoric sense of flying. John crawled up behind me, and together we sat on top, holding each other, too exhausted to speak.

I told myself several times, *Remember this moment. Remember what it is like. Later in my life, years from now, I will look back, many times, on this scene; this day will stand above all.*

But I could not appreciate it. I was only thankful at the moment to rest, to breathe and lessen the dizziness, and if I felt anything akin to elation, it was from the realization I no longer had to go up. This was it; there was no higher place to climb.

# The Challenge of El Capitan

## Chris Bonington

*Chris Bonington is a leading international climber and author of numerous books, including* Mountaineer *and* Quest for Adventure, *from which this piece is taken.*

The greatest challenge of all was to free climb the Nose. The 1980s, with rising rock-climbing standards around the world, saw many routes going free that had originally been climbed using extensive aid, and 1980 saw the first serious free attempt on the Nose by Ray Jardine. He was the inventor of the Friend, an adjustable camming device that revolutionized protection in wide parallel cracks. The main crux was the completely blank section above the top of El Cap Tower. Jardine chiseled a sparse line of holds to link the two lines of weakness, but the Great Roof defeated him. Repeated insertion and removal of chrome molybdenum pegs in the thin crack snaking up the side of the huge overhang had left widened pockets into which fingers that were not too large could just fit, but it was too much for Jardine.

Thirteen more years passed before the Nose was climbed free in its entirety, although there were plenty of attempts. It was a trip not so much into the geographical, as into the athletic and personal unknown, and in many ways the journey epitomizes the challenge and dilemma of the modern adventurer when all the obvious geographical firsts have been attained. Lynn Hill found the solution, and in doing so she not only established herself as the best woman rock climber in the world but also broke through the sex barrier, emerging as one of the best, if not *the* best, all-round rock climbers in history.

At only five foot one, she made up for lack of height with a superb power-to-weight ratio, gymnastic ability, and, most important, focus of mind. Born in 1961, she had a traditional apprenticeship that inevitably took her to Yosemite for an ascent of the Nose and other test pieces. One of her climbing partners was John Long, who had made the first ascent of the Nose in a day.

She visited Europe for the first time in 1986, at the invitation of French climbers, and was impressed by the standards that had been developed on the limestone walls of southern France. Sport climbing, as it has come to be known, using bolts for protection but climbing the rock without using any aid, had progressed to a high level. In a way it was a retreat from adventure, because the element of risk had been minimized to allow the climber to develop his or her athletic skill to the ultimate. It also marked the birth of formalized competition climbing. Lynn Hill was invited to Bardonecchia in Italy for one of the early competitions. She was the only American there, it was all strange to her, but she ended up very nearly winning, being runner-up to Catherine Destivelle from France.

These two women dominated the burgeoning competition-climbing circuit for the next few years. Their successes gave them the means of earning a very good living around the activity they loved and enabled them to stretch their skills to the limit and reach the clearly defined summit of that sport. Both, however, grew tired of the limitations of competition climbing, always indoors on artificial walls with the pressure of intensive training. Each returned to traditional adventure climbing. Destivelle made a series of remarkable ascents in the high mountains, which included a solo new route on the

Southwest Pillar of the Dru and an ascent, with Jeff Lowe, of a new route on the Trango Tower in the Karakoram. Lynn Hill, meanwhile, returned to Yosemite and the challenge of the Nose of El Capitan.

While climbing at Cave Rock near Lake Tahoe, she happened to meet up with Simon Nadin, a British climber who had also been on the competition circuit, becoming first-ever world champion at the 1989 finals in Leeds. He, like Lynn, came from a traditional climbing background and like her had returned to it. When they discovered that they both were intrigued by the challenge of climbing the Nose free, Simon postponed his return flight to Britain and three days later they were in Yosemite.

They reached the foot of the Great Roof on their third day without incident, but they were beginning to feel the fatigue from not only free climbing 2,000 feet but also hauling their provisions and carrying a heavy rack of nuts and camming devices. Lynn commented: "After climbing from 5:30 A.M. until midnight the previous day, I had gained a great respect for the amount of time and energy the route demanded. The force of gravity seemed to multiply the higher we climbed."

They were sharing the lead and Simon had first try on the Great Roof pitch but quickly backed off. It was now Lynn's turn. She laybacked up the sheer open corner, the tips of her fingers barely fitting into the thin crack, to where the roof thrust out above her. This was the crux, with a series of tenuous undercut holds in the back of the bulging overhang and even more tenuous smears on the granite wall for her feet. She was nearly at the end when she miscalculated a move. Her foot slipped and she was off, hurtling headfirst toward the ground 2,000 feet below. Ironically, the very steepness and smoothness of the wall was her protection, and she dangled unhurt at the end of the rope. Her running belay had held and Simon lowered her to the ledge.

She was now very tired, realizing that she had used up almost all her energy, but she was determined to have just one more try. Lynn summoned what reserves she had, this time pushing beyond her previous high point, reaching for the very last hold, when her foot slid off what was no more than a smear. Miraculously, her head touched the roof just at the right moment to enable her to maintain equilibrium, and she propelled herself on. She extended her arm as far as she could and reached her fingers into a small undercling lock. After a few relatively straightforward moves, she was on the ledge to join some Croatian climbers who were tackling the route by conventional means.

Next morning she and Simon shared their last morsels of food, half an energy bar and a date each, and then set out on their fourth day with some hard climbing ahead. Simon led the notorious pitch around the Glowering Spot, so named by Warren Harding because he had broken his hammer there in a particularly awkward bit of aid climbing and there is a lump of rock that looks like a grumpy face.

Lynn was hoping to conserve her diminishing stock of energy for the final extreme section just above Camp VI, where others had tried and failed. It was reputed to be very blank, needing a long reach, something that Lynn most certainly did not have. A brief investigation was enough to reveal no intermediate holds. The way Harding had originally gone was up a sheer groove to the right with a hairline crack in its back. Just getting into it was desperate. At its base was a pocket where she might have gotten a finger lock, but it was filled by the stub of an old broken-off piton. She tried virtually everything, trying to brace herself in the smooth, flared, holdless corner, but she could make no upward progress and eventually admitted defeat, using aid to complete the climb and reach the top.

But she could not let it go and constantly thought of ways and means of solving this seemingly impossible problem. Sponsorship crept into the equation, but in an indirect kind of way. One of her sponsors was so impressed by her free ascent of the Great Roof, a major achievement in its own right, that they wanted her to repeat it in front of a professional photographer in order to get some really good advertising shots. She could do this and try to complete the section that had defeated her earlier.

She invited Brooke Sandahl, who had been exploring free-climbing possibilities on the upper part of the Nose the previous year, to join her. They started by abseiling in from the top to investigate and, to a degree, prepare the critical pitch above Camp VI. Lynn removed the broken-off piton, to free up a hold to start with, and then spent three days trying out various permutations of moves to climb the pitch. "As I became engrossed in exploring unusual techniques and body positions on this pitch, I was increasingly appreciative of its extraordinary nature. Climbing it free would involve an ingenuity and technical finesse that I rarely, if ever, encountered on any other route." Lynn eventually managed to complete the pitch with only one fall, but she felt that to claim the entire climb as a free ascent, she had to start at the bottom and go all the way to the top.

This time she and her partner had more food and slipped into a better rhythm, enabling Lynn to lead the Great Roof in a single push. They pressed on past Camp V and up the pitch round the Glowering Spot, which this time she led. They reached Camp VI and got a good night's sleep before the final challenge. She dreamed of the moves that night, and the following morning it all came together as if in the dream. The final pitch, casting to left and right for tenuous holds to either side of Harding's bolt ladder, led them to the top and the completion of a climb that established Lynn Hill's position as one of the most extraordinary rock climbers of all time.

But this achievement still wasn't quite enough for her. Could she complete the climb in a day? It wasn't so much to make a speed record as to climb it in the most elegant way possible, to travel light without the need of hauling food and water. "It not only represented a kind of marathon linkage of this monumental route but provided a new focus and evolution in my life."

Her climbing partner was to be Steve Sutton, who was happy to take on the role of belayer, jumaring all the way up the route. His role was similar to that of a caddie to a top professional golfer. He was even being paid. Lynn welcomed the encouragement he gave her. On her first attempt she made the mistake of coproducing a documentary film of her ascent and, not surprisingly, found she was losing that very focus she sought. By the time she reached the Great Roof after 22 pitches of climbing, she had run out of chalk and nearly run out of water. She was tired and flustered, and after five attempts and five and a half hours' struggle, they completed the climb using aid.

She was back again a fortnight later, this time without filming commitments and fully focused on the climb ahead. They started at 10 P.M., climbing in the ethereal light of a full moon, and were at the Great Roof by 8:30 in the morning. She took a rest, dozed for what seemed no time at all, but suddenly realized that the sun was creeping round the corner. It was vital to climb the Great Roof while it was still cool. This time she made the daunting pitch in a single push, laybacking the open corner to the roof with an easy rhythmic movement, placing the occasional nut, and clipping into in-situ pitons. Then, as she came to the overhang with its tiny undercut holds, she had a moment of self-doubt. To save energy, she hadn't bothered to clip a piton just below, and suddenly she realized that if she did fall, she'd swing hard into the corner. She thrust away the moment of doubt, focused on the rock in front of her, and took each move steadily, to pull out onto the ledge at 10:25.

The day was getting even hotter. Pitch followed pitch. The next major challenge was the Glowering Spot, which she reached at midday. She was beginning to tire and her hands were sweaty. She'd reached the hard moves and placed a stopper (small metal wedge) in the crack, but before she had time to seat it, it slipped out. She didn't have another of the right size. If she had fallen, she would have hit the ledge some 30 feet below. She kept cool, found another placement for one of her two remaining pieces of gear, and pulled up and over the crux to easier ground.

At only one o'clock in the afternoon she reached Camp VI, but the hardest pitch of all was ahead. The holds in the open groove were so tenuous she needed the rock to be as cool as possible for better friction for her climbing shoes and the complex pressure holds she would be using. She tried to doze through the afternoon, waiting for the groove to go into the shade. She waited four and a half hours but, impatient to get going, started before the rock had had time to cool and, as a result, had her first fall. The moves were complex, convoluted, and tenuous, requiring precise body balance and muscular pressure. She got it wrong and again went hurtling down. She rested on the belay, refocusing and trying to keep the doubt from sliding into her mind, but she was getting tired. This third attempt could be her last chance. She started up the complex opening moves again but had not even got as high as on her previous attempt before her foot slipped and she was off once more. It wasn't life threatening; she could afford to fall, but she had put in so much effort.

Lynn went into the fourth attempt. She concentrated everything she had on those next moves. This was the concentration of the Olympic athlete going for gold, but she had no audience, just the huge void below and a smooth, sheer, rounded arête in front that she was pinching with her fingers as she frictioned her feet precariously up its edge. This time she made it, reached a positive hold, and pulled up to the belay ledge.

She still had four pitches to climb. The last two were difficult and strenuous, although not as hard as the one she had just completed. The top pitch—the section on which Harding had hammered a bolt ladder—gave a last challenge with the final overhang. She knew her reserves of strength were very nearly finished. She made one last dynamic, irreversible lunge for the final hold on the final roof and caught it. She heaved and swung up onto the easy slabs that led to the top of the Nose. She had achieved her objective, 33 rope lengths, more than 3,000 feet of supremely hard climbing in just 23 hours.

Lynn Hill used her finely tuned self-discipline to perfect the climb, in effect making a new and fresh route, arguably the longest and most difficult free rock climb in the world.

# Climbing Frozen Waterfalls

## David Ferrell

A frozen waterfall is a slick seductress, fragile and breathtaking.

To climb the face of one—to shinny up all 600 feet of Colorado's Ames Ice Hose, for example—is to skate on the razor edge of disaster.

The ice is fickle, sometimes weakened by sunlight, or corroded by trapped air. Or frozen so brittle it shatters in face-stinging shards under the force of an ice ax.

Halfway up elegant glassy pillars and overhanging chandeliers, any number of things can go wrong, from mind-numbing fatigue and cramps to high winds and avalanches. A broken prong on a boot once sent Alex Lowe free falling 170 feet before his safety rope slammed him into the cliff, knocking him unconscious and driving a pick into his hand. Michael O'Donnell was overtaken one year by a winter storm; he surrendered four toes to frostbite and lost his climbing partner, who died of exhaustion and hypothermia.

There are icicles 50 feet long, weighing thousands of pounds apiece. Ice climber John Bouchard remembers scaling the crest of one just as the whole formation gave way; he ended up dangling over a 2,800-foot chasm with two broken ribs.

"If you do it hard for 15 years, you've got a 50 percent chance of dying . . . maybe 30 percent," Bouchard, 45, said of the sport, carefully examining his estimate in light of a dozen or so friends killed while climbing and mountaineering over the years. "But not me," he added, laughing defiantly. "Not me!"

He mocks death, laughs in its face, and others of his ilk laugh in a chorus all around him. Bouchard and the multiplying legions of ice climbers are part of an expanding universe of extreme athletes, men and women who embrace great risk and sometimes excruciating pain to satisfy a craving for thrills, glory, or the quiet satisfaction that comes of struggle and triumph.

In every era there are daredevils—jungle explorers and mountain trekkers, tightrope walkers who bridge the gulf between skyscrapers, solo sailors who point themselves over Niagara in a barrel—but today the cultural landscape has changed. Technology and market forces have squeezed the sporting world into a high-action, hard-wired video loop. So overwhelming is the multichanneled deluge of events and images that the only way to create a flash, to capture the restless eye of notoriety, is to somehow exceed the boundaries of normal human achievement.

To some that means jumping from an airplane on a surfboard, surfing a few thousand feet of open sky before pulling the rip cord. Or it means skiing off mountain ledges onto 70-degree slopes, or mashing the gas to send a 1,400-horsepower monster truck careening through midair. Or it means pushing the flesh to the farthest limits of endurance in 100-mile ultramarathons and 300-mile "adventure races" across the rutted mountains and rivers of Patagonia and South Africa.

Whole subcultures have evolved: hugely muscled arena gladiators, speed-freak mountain-bike racers and asphalt lugers, nomadic competitors who earn fleeting moments of cable television fame on the lumberjack and demolition derby circuits.

The sport of waterfall ice climbing, a winter spinoff of rock climbing, did not even exist until the late '60s, when alpinist Yvon Chouinard began experimenting with curved ax picks that could grip a sheer ice surface. From a few thousand early devotees, ice climbing has spiraled into a worldwide passion practiced anywhere that freezing rivers rain and glaciers pour off cliffs and down through craggy ravines.

Thousands of known routes are now assaulted every winter by hard-core climbers who number upward of 100,000, said Jeff Lowe (no relation to Alex), a pioneer who was part of a seminal moment 23 years ago when he and Mike Weis trudged into a snowy, white-peaked valley near Telluride, Colorado. What they did was struggle up the face of frozen Bridal Veil Falls, a stunning, 330-foot stream of dripping candle wax, a feat so riveting that it inspired the first wave of big-time ice climbers.

The real boom, however, has come in the last five years, as evidenced by the extensive coverage in *Rock & Ice* and *Climbing* magazines, by men's and women's ice-climbing events at ESPN's new Winter Extreme Games, and the advent of the nation's first ice-climbing recreational park: a half-mile-long, artificially irrigated gorge in Ouray, Colorado.

"For people in the industry, there's been a surge of prosperity they never expected or really even hoped for," said Terry Hersher, a former ice climber who owns a shop called Telluride Mountaineer in the Colorado Rockies, one of the hubs of waterfall climbing in America.

"Going back a couple of years, ice climbers were a very small, easily identifiable group. Today, there are a lot more urban people . . . people from Los Angeles, Seattle. Typically, they're very capable, competent individuals . . . in general very intelligent."

Men far outnumber women, but the sport's growth has occurred along a wide age range—from teenagers to men in their 40s and 50s, many of them rock-climbing veterans out to fill the winter months. Some are regular working stiffs, exploiting weekends and vacations to climb, while a good number are devoted outdoorsmen who make a living as wilderness guides, owners of mountaineering shops, even designers of name-brand climbing gear.

What they share is often an obsession with the ice and its astonishing beauty.

Climbers talk at length about the gelid wonders they see, crystal castles, great fairylands of icicles, pools, fluted glass figurines, undulating masses that vary in size and color, frosty white, transparent, tinted with the rusty brown of leeching iron, the luminous blue of flowing water.

"Six inches from your face you can just marvel at the way the icicles have formed. [The ice] is different depending on the amount of air that froze into it and the speed of the water as it was frozen," said Scott Ayers, who traveled to well-known climbing spots in Colorado, the Canadian Rockies, and the Andes to produce a video, *On Ice,* which he markets in climbing magazines.

"There are vertical things that look like the tentacles of a squid or octopus. You're climbing up into those and they're as beautiful as they are terrifying. To me, it's like walking into an art gallery and looking at the most beautiful paintings in the world."

Bridal Veil is one such showcase, its waxy tumble of ice featuring one milky blue column that is especially compelling. Clinging to its writhing surface 200 feet up, a climber can see through to the water still flowing inside.

"It's like climbing up to a window or a television screen and looking in," marveled Greg Child, 39, who traveled to Bridal Veil this month to climb in a place where winter ice is still abundant. "What you can see, a few feet back, is . . . the waterfall actually rushing inside the ice. It's a bizarre thing."

The water pipe is not only surreal but a frightful bit of plumbing this time of year, when the ice is growing thinner. Crack it with an ax and freezing water gushes out. Climber Antoine Savelli, who has done just that, has a nightmare that the entire column will collapse beneath him.

"The fear," he said, "is that the ice will break away and you'll fall [inside the pipe] and drown."

As yet, no one has suffered that misfortune, but danger is integral to the experience, wrapping itself around the beauty in a yin-yang way that climbers find mesmerizing. They are moved to poetry; they speak of attaining extraordinary focus while suspended on 1,000-foot, limestone cliffs, becoming locked in Zen-like states of consciousness.

"It's a mystical experience," said Savelli, 40, a lithe climber who has scaled mountain peaks throughout Europe and the United States. "The actual act of climbing is so immediate . . . addicting. It never fades."

In the teeth of great risk, the cares of past and future disengage and slip away, leaving only a present so vivid it fairly shimmers before the eyes—a "hyper-reality" comparable to an out-of-body experience, according to some psychologists. Skydivers get the same mental clarity, said James H. Frey, a sports sociologist at the University of Nevada at Las Vegas who studied the mind-set in the late 1980s.

Far from being crazy or out of control, the daredevils of extreme sports are often relatively conservative thinkers motivated by mankind's eternal desire to conquer obstacles, to win recognition, Frey said. In the skies or on the ice, they may push their limits farther and farther, but at home and on the job they tend to minimize risks. They spend frugally. They wear seat belts. They seldom smoke. The Zeitgeist is one of well-exercised control.

"Even in the most extremely dangerous situations . . . the [thrill seeker] feels that he or she is in control," Frey said. "They have

the proper equipment, the proper training, they've prepared themselves mentally and physically, and they feel they should be able to
accomplish the feat—to jump out of an airplane or climb the waterfall or whatever they happen to be doing."

That notion is partly delusional. One characteristic of ice
climbing, in particular, is the existence of objective hazards—situations beyond the borders of a climber's skill. Savelli's latest brush with
an objective hazard happened in February on the Ice Hose, a great
downward blast of ice that dominates a pine-covered cliff a few miles
from Bridal Veil. He was about a third of the way up—200 feet off
the canyon floor—when an avalanche began.

Avalanches follow the same natural contours as running
water; this one came straight down the Hose.

"I heard a roar at first and looked up and saw this white
thing fanning out above me," Savelli said. He pulled himself
against the cliff, hoping that anything hard or heavy would fly over
his head. It did, but enough light powder got him to nearly knock
him off.

Telling the story, Savelli grinned, basking in the jittery after-
glow of it. That is the other pole that draws climbers to frozen water-
falls. During the times in between the Zen states, during those idle
night hours spent sipping brandy in the firelight, there are stories to
tell—commonalities of experience that solidify friendships, hoary
ascents that scrape the shine off a man, earning him passage into an
elite fraternity.

"There's a social dimension to risk," as Frey pointed out.
"The group is very important to them, and the group sets the
norms . . . for performance. Status in the group is defined by your
success as a climber . . . and as you climb key climbs, your status in
the group goes up."

Spectators are seldom seen; ice climbing is a notoriously solitary act, a retreat in which even two climbing partners are separated
on the face of the falls. But within the subculture, personal achieve-

ments are well chronicled, and stars enjoy a fame spread via magazine layouts and Internet gossip.

Important routes are often christened by the first to conquer them; hence, a Tolkienesque geography of ice sheets whose names conjure both awe and dread: Wowie-Zowie in Valdez, Alaska; Casket Quarry outside Duluth, Minnesota; the Fang in Vail, Colorado; Wicked Wanda and the Weeping Wall in the immense climbing cathedrals of the Canadian Rockies; Gorillas in the Mist in the Adirondack Mountains of New York.

Unlike a rock cliff, an ice route is ever changing and ephemeral, forming up fat one year, thin the next, wriggling and shedding even day to day under the onslaught of rain and snow, wind and sun.

Subzero temperatures in December and January can turn the ice as brittle as bone china. An ax will tend to shatter it into flat fragments, "dinner plates" that rattle a climber's helmet and mark his face with cuts and bruises.

Toward the season's end—March and April in much of North America—conditions are more hospitable. The cold is not so bitter and the ice becomes "plastic," an ideal state easy to penetrate with the ax. Paradoxically, the danger often escalates during this time. Immense ice spears and anvils loosen; meltwater drives an insidious wedge between the face of a cliff and tons of frozen water that wait to come crashing down.

"You can almost do a mental countdown of how long you can hang on before the ice starts to melt and disintegrate," said Child, an Australian who has scaled Everest.

Ice climbing is accomplished with two axes—one in each hand—and a rack of metal prongs, crampons affixed to each boot. A climber literally crawls, hand over hand, up a vertical face, sinking the ax with every step. A good climber travels a 150-foot rope length in half an hour or less, but glassy chandeliers and overhanging ice can make progress infinitely tedious. A hard climb can take hours, even most of a day.

It is arduous work. The forearms burn. The hands become numb and frozen—"like clubs," one climber said. An exhausted climber, stuck in the middle of a 200-foot falls, may fear dropping an ax and so tighten his wrist leashes, worsening the numbness in his hands. His technique may deteriorate, costing more energy to make only the most meager progress.

"You'll find yourself too weak to pull out your ax, and then too weak to hold it over your head, let alone put it back in the ice," said Dan Michalee, 40, a Chicago dental technician who began ice climbing just a year ago. "I see people . . . hitting anything, just throwing their ax up there hoping it hits and sticks. And usually it won't."

Climbers call it thrashing. It is a sign of poor judgment at a time climber's axes pull out and he falls.

The trouble is, no single act is quite so likely to cause a slip as stopping to install such a screw. The climber must first let go an ax. Then, with a gloved, frozen hand, he must align the screw without dropping it—each one costs $40 to $65—and twist it into the ice even while he clings like an insect to the sheer waterfall surface on two pairs of toe prongs and his remaining ax.

As Michalee pointed out, the very fact that he is installing a screw means the climber is probably far above the last screw he placed; a mistake, therefore, might send him plummeting 100 feet or more before his rope saves him—assuming he put in the last screw properly.

Into the calculation about where screws should be placed goes the time factor. The longer it takes to ascend to the top, the greater the odds that sections of the falls may collapse.

"Speed is sometimes safer than more protection," Michalee said.

Those who excel at the sport are often in peerless shape, relishing the test of strength and willpower.

"Ice climbing is retrospectively pleasurable," said Alex Lowe, 38, one of the world's best, a man his peers call "The Mutant" because of his uncanny endurance. "It's not necessarily a good time every minute you're doing it. It's cold and you're scared and all that. It's not a sport of the masses. Most people don't want to suffer.

"But to me, that [suffering] increases the satisfaction of doing it. When you stand back and look at the collective event, it's good."

Mental toughness is essential. Lowe, who lives in Boseman, Montana, with his ice-climbing wife and three young boys, is known for doing 400 pull-ups a day and rigging a bungee cord to a door handle in his car to give his arms a workout while he drives. After an ice fragment fell in his eye during a climb in Cody, Wyoming, slicing his cornea and ruining his once-perfect vision, he had difficulty understanding why a writer found it worth noting in *Climbing* magazine.

"That's sort of incidental," he said, downplaying the dangers with a bit of philosophy. "I'm not a risk taker, I'm a risk controller. I don't have a death wish. I have a life wish."

Ice-climbing deaths are rare—only one or two a year in North America, according to the American Alpine Club—but injuries are common. They usually occur during falls that might be far worse except for ropes and safety screws. Climbers tend to slam into the sides of cliffs, getting stabbed with their own axes or catching their crampons in the ice while free falling, a misstep guaranteed to twist or break an ankle.

Medical help is usually miles away. In its annual report on mountaineering accidents, a terse, matter-of-fact publication that in spite of itself tends to read like a synopsis of Wile E. Coyote misadventures, the American Alpine Club noted one case of a climber who slipped last year while 45 feet up icy Cannon Cliff in New Hampshire.

Two safety screws gave way and the climber crashed to the ground, breaking two bones in his right leg and another in his left shoulder. His only immediate assistance came from two partners who put a splint on his leg and tied his helmet to his foot so he could more easily drag his broken leg over the snow.

In that fashion the climber "crawled feet-first down the snow-covered talus slope and then at times head-first through the trees," the report said. "The crawl to the road took four hours."

Horror stories like that have made some agencies and private property owners wary of ice climbers. At Denali National Park in Alaska, climbers are now being charged a $150 usage fee—the original plan was $500—to help offset the cost of the many mountain rescues performed by volunteer rangers. The money is a sore point to many climbers, who point out that campers, hunters, and fishermen pay no such fees in spite of the burden they place on rescuers.

"Hunters get lost all the time," Jeff Lowe said. "There's just an outcry against climbers because a lot of people don't understand climbers and they think they're crazy."

A nonprofit climbers group called the Access Fund, founded in 1991, has struggled to smooth out the inevitable conflicts that occur as climbers sally forth into remote lands controlled by the government or private owners. The group's biggest triumph occurred this winter with the reopening of Bridal Veil, a falls closed off for many years because of private property holdings. After Jeff Lowe's first ascent, climbing there virtually ceased except for the occasional zealots who, according to legend, sneaked up it at night like thieves.

Climbers have gained a greater degree of legitimacy in recent years, and growing ranks of beginners have nudged it toward the mainstream, but its hard-core factions are still pushing the limits.

Bouchard is one. He suggests that there is a powerful satisfaction in confronting danger and hardship and performing well, the way he was forced to rally after that 50-foot icicle collapsed beneath him in the Andes. With two broken ribs, he climbed several hundred feet before reaching an overnight camp.

He experienced a similar kind of duress during his historic first ascent of the 600-foot Black Dike in New Hampshire in 1971, when his rope tangled and he was forced to drop it.

"For four hours I climbed about 200 feet where every move I made was the hardest move I ever made," Bouchard said. "I didn't climb for about a month afterward."

But that was long ago. Now, he is planning his next big trip: a summer excursion to the North Pillar of Latok, an 8,000-foot ascent that ends at an elevation of 24,000 feet in the Pakistani Himalayas.

Top-echelon ice climbers see the Himalayas as the final frontier: the world's greatest mountains, immense, frozen places where the ice and rock chase each other into the sky for miles, uncharted territory far and wide. Child pictures himself there someday, no rope, no protection, the whole world spinning beneath him.

"Maybe . . . reaching out with your ice tools and chipping in by a couple of millimeters into a goatee of ice . . . 25,000 feet . . . and you swing around on that ice ax and you look down and all you can see are your crampons swinging around in the breeze. That really excites me," he said. "That kind of climbing is what I dream of being able to do."

# Big-Mountain Freeskiing

## Mark Peruzzi

*Marc Peruzzi is an assistant editor for* Outside *magazine, from which this piece is taken.*

Trying to look nonchalant while your dislocated shoulder unleashes waves of dizzying pain can be, well, trying. Mine's a trick shoulder, prone to popping out on the wet side of Eskimo rolls and other times when it's nice to have a contiguous skeletal system. Like right now. I'm standing at the base of a 46-degree slope stretching 1,000 feet up Mount Alyeska above Girdwood, Alaska. It's March 22, day one of the Red Bull Snowthrill—the finale of the International Free Skiers Association's 2000 world tour—and I'd rather not introduce myself to "50 of the world's bravest freeskiers," as the press release puts it, by doing the funky chicken. So as my pole pierces the snowpack and my shoulder wrenches loose, I stifle a yelp and wait for bone to ferret back to socket.

Which it does, as soon as I'm able to focus on someone else's pain. High above, Sarah Newman, of Mount Hutt, New Zealand, has dead-ended on a spit of snow with only two means of escape: a 25-foot cliff drop or a disgraceful hike back uphill. After staring at her landing for three long minutes, Newman suicide-shoves off the edge, with all the grace of a carp. Plopping sideways in the soft snow, she spins, falls backward over another 25-footer, and starfishes through scattered rock before coming to a halt minus a ski. Miraculously, she's unhurt.

The uninitiated observer might assume that such NASCAR-style corporeal pileups are part of the show, but when I look around I see there are no other spectators. The IFSA tour was formed to reward the creativity, technical brilliance, and aggressiveness that have branded big-mountain freeskiing the sport's most audacious discipline. And yet, here at the Snowthrill, they've taken an activity defined by the infinite possibilities offered up in a giant, untamed pyramid of snow and tried to package it in the form of a contest.

Problem is, it ain't working. Mother Nature doesn't compromise, especially in the Chugach Range. By 2 P.M., the mountains are living up to their temperamental reputation. Just up above Jim's Rock, a two-story boulder wedged near the crest of the ridge, stands the official Red Bull starting gate: a 15-foot-tall foam billboard emblazoned with two of the trademark bloodred, seemingly hairless devil-bulls about to lock horns. No sooner has the first round been completed than a gust of wind knocks the starting gate off its moorings, and the bulls find themselves in a thousand-foot slide for life. It's guiltless carnage to be sure. Straight-running through the rocks, the beasts catch 40 feet of air off a boulder—attempting a back flip, perhaps, but fatally under-rotating. The billboard explodes on impact, the bits and pieces rocket-glissading downslope with a ski patrolman and photographer in frantic Keystone Cops pursuit.

As the broken bulls self-arrest, the clouds start spitting flakes. Over on the judging stand, somebody from Mountain Sports International (the event organizers hired by IFSA and Red Bull to put on the Snowthrill) announces over the P.A. that the second run is canceled. A storm is rolling in. It is highly ironic, but fresh powder is bad news for big-mountain events: low-to-no visibility means judges can't see the skiers and skiers can't see the rocks. But for the rest of us, it's a powder day. Everybody—competitors, resort guests, locals—takes off to ski the lower mountain. The Snowthrill sits idle as the clouds dump for the next seven days.

If you've ever felt weightless floating through dry snow on a run you could ski by moonlight, you have an inkling of what freeskiing is. It's skiing without trails, or crowds, or tracks. It's flowing downhill fast, like water, a solitary affair between skier and mountain. The semantic nuances that differentiate "big-mountain freeskiing" from "extreme skiing" might seem negligible to someone who has never done either, but they're not. True extreme skiing in the French tradition takes place on the 60-degree, if-you-fall-you-die ice of technical ski mountaineering; big-mountain freeskiing is about going fast on more forgiving alpine faces with 2,000 vertical feet of powder, catching air where appropriate. In essence, surfing the mountain. It's why people quit their jobs and move to Alta for a decade or two. And it has nothing to do with judges, sponsors, or sports drinks.

By 1996, "extreme"-ism was popping up everywhere. In North America, where the skiing public generally couldn't give a rat's ass about alpine racing, ski manufacturers were employing it as a marketing catchphrase to boost lagging sales in an industry that hadn't seen innovation since the hot dog movement of the mid-1970s (think red-white-and-blue nylon ski pants, headbands, and the "Worm Turn"). When he founded the International Free Skiers Association that year, Shane McConkey, an amateur freeskier who had won the 1995 U.S. National Extreme Skiing championships and was eking out a living appearing in ski films, was not only protesting the co-optation of the word "extreme" but trying to show respect for the people who had called themselves "freeskiers" for 20 years. Word about his brainchild percolated through the freeskiing community via www.freeskiers.org and various ski magazines, and by the 2000 season IFSA had an office in Park City, Utah, and over 1,000 dues-paying members.

Although McConkey changed the name, big-mountain freeskiing contests are organized in the same way as extreme skiing events. Competitors' runs are evaluated by a panel of judges who assign 1 to 10 points each for line selection, control, fluidity, technique, and aggressiveness. At the Snowthrill, organizers allowed seven days to get in three runs—two on the ridgeline connecting Mount Alyeska to Max's Mountain, rising nearly 4,000 feet from sea level just west of Turnagain Arm, and one on bigger and steeper mountains in the Chugach backcountry. Worst-case scenario: Two runs would suffice to decide the championship.

Of course, the basic premise of awarding points to something as subjective as freeskiing is absurd. To judge it objectively, you'd need to make everybody ski the same line, time them, and mark the distance they travel off the same jump—in effect, killing the "free" in freeskiing. Since the IFSA doesn't go that far (there's no precise measurement; judges decide how many points to assign a skier based on their own criteria), it creates an inherent contradiction. Put it this way: Tiger Woods is the world's best golfer because he dominates the PGA, but is the IFSA tour champ really the best?

"I meet clients from Minnesota who are as good as anyone," says Dean Cummings, lead guide for Valdez H2O, an Alaskan heli-skiing outfit, and the 1995 World Extreme Skiing champ. The IFSA tour, he says, "is a point system—they're crowning the guy with the resources and time to get to the most events." Cummings, who still runs WESC, isn't just griping. The fact is that most big-name freeskiers making a living in the pucker zone (read "the steep terrain that shrinks your sphincter") don't bother entering IFSA events. McConkey, for example, couldn't make it to Snowthrill this year because he was making a video in Europe for Match Stick Productions; other well-known film freeskiers like Seth Morrison, Kent Kreitler, and Wendy Fisher have abandoned the tour altogether. Jeremy Nobis, 30, a Teton Gravity Research film star, deigned to attend Snowthrill, but as a judge, not a competitor. The only high-profile skiers who showed up were 1996 World Extreme Skiing Champion (and Red Bull–sponsored athlete) Chris Davenport, 29, and 1998 Extreme Skiing women's champ Francine Moreillon, 31. The crux? What was originally conceived as a tour to reward the strongest and most versatile skiers has become a series of over-regulated one-rock huckfests featuring about 150—how to put it?—less-skilled athletes. (The Snowthrill itself was only able to attract 21 men and 9 women, hardly the 50 that Red Bull had promised.)

McConkey, 30, acknowledges the problems but doesn't have a quick fix. "Four years ago, our sport needed structuring," he says. "Now we've gone overboard with too many rules and regulations. I'd like to change things around, keep it fun." Then he adds: "People eat shit all the time, but it's like that in all these sports. You go to a surfing event and you see people who suck. These events are a means to an end for a lot of skiers."

A pretty meager means, actually. Skiers at Snowthrill paid a $650 entry fee to compete, not to mention their own travel expenses. Out of a $15,000 purse, the men's and women's winners get $5,000 apiece, leaving the second and third finishers in each division to fight over the scraps. Everyone else goes away hungry. Not a whole lot for risking your life.

But then, it's never really been about the money. When I asked Chris Davenport, who finished second overall on the 2000 IFSA tour (despite skipping two events), what pure big-mountain freeskiing is all about, he recounted a scene he and Wendy Fisher witnessed while waiting in line at the Whistler Peak Chair in 1999. Nothing huge, just a local guy negotiating a short but technical cliff run called Air Jordan, which involved an 8- to 10-foot drop onto a 45-degree hanging face, followed by a 15-foot drop off a second cliff. "[The guy] just drops in straight runs, and sticks the second landing, making nice turns through the trees," said Davenport. "Our jaws dropped. The best freeskier in the world couldn't have made it look any better."

The guy was Brett Carlson, a Whistler local who had never really made a go of it on the freeskiing tour like his best friend, 1999 IFSA Tour Champion Jeff Holden. To hear Davenport and Holden tell it, Carlson was the real deal. He and Holden had honed their skills in the British Columbia backcountry and became known for hucking monster cliffs, once successfully dropping a 100-foot wall dubbed The Doctor. But Holden was also there on January 17 of this year, when Carlson, 24, tried to jump a two-lane road outside Whistler. He came up short and died the moment his body hit the pavement. A month after the accident, Holden retreated to the Kootenai backcountry to get his head together. Already suffering from microtears in his back due to a car wreck, he tore the meniscus in his knee and is now trying to regroup.

"I'm stoked to be in the mountains this year and see where they take me," says Holden, 25. Still, Carlson's death is never far away. "That jump was doable," Holden says. "Maybe [the snow] needed to set up more, maybe it just wasn't the right time—there are a lot of maybes. . . . It's made me more interested in doing my homework. I never did my homework in school because the facts didn't add up to anything. But on the mountain, studying, researching, dialing lines in, it results in that creation, that flow."

The tram stinks. It smells like Sunday morning in a college dorm john. My goggles are fogging, and I'm elbow-to-elbow with 30 swamp-assed skiers sweating out Red Bull and vodka and whispering about powder stashes.

I'm home.

The tram is taking us up Alyeska's steep and deep north face, but aside from the fact that everyone's clutching chubby Alaskan skis instead of 205-centimeter slalom boards, this aerial cattle car is pretty much indistinguishable from the tram at Cannon Mountain, New Hampshire, where I spent the best part of my early 20s. I was in college then. The school had a great racing program, but my friends and I weren't there to bash gates. Our thing was heading out in groups of

20 or more, raging down the bumps, hollering through the trees. We never gave it much thought, but we were freeskiers.

Though I'm sardined with card-carrying IFSA members, they're not much different. They're certainly not overly concerned with the official program or the fact that the competition has been postponed for two days. They've got their priorities. To wit: about 30 inches of wet, untracked fresh below. When the doors open and everyone goes right, I go left, adhering to skiing's number-one rule: There are no friends on a powder day.

Unfortunately, I don't know my way around. So out on the face, I employ rule number two: Hook up with a local. He's side-stepping to a high traverse that leads to Christmas and New Years chutes, two 46-degree couloirs that haven't been opened at the top because of avalanche danger but can be accessed safely a little way down. We pole along for 10 minutes before dropping into Christmas and then whip-turning up to the ridge.

My guide quickly descends through a line of firs, and I'm left alone above a steep spine that drops into a shallow gully. It's a swell of snow hanging perhaps 48 degrees at its steepest point; I ride it like a wave, letting my skis accelerate down its face before arcing a bottom turn and heading back upslope. I smear-turn on the lip, powder spills into my mouth, and an undertow of slough threatens to take me out at the ankles just as I drop from the crest into the tube and do it all over again. Traditional skis would nose-dive in this heavy snow, but not these fat boys. I'm floating.

The next three days are a blur of tram runs and ever-deeper snow. But after a week of almost constant snowfall and milk-bottle visibility, my legs have had about as much as they can handle. At breakfast on the last day, a message board at the Westin Alyeska Resort buffet line informs the assembled horde that the event is on again, albeit on milder, lift-served terrain. A patch of blue sky has opened long enough for the ski patrol to bomb the north face, and most of the skiers are already out inspecting the course. When I get there, I see a brand-new Red Bull starting gate standing strong on a knob above Christmas and New Years chutes.

At about 1 P.M., the first skier comes down. Aiming directly for a minefield of rock looming at 50 degrees over the gullet of Christmas chute, he punches his hands forward to accelerate and, without moving his tips from the fall line, knocks off three butter-smooth turns on vertical scraps of snow, floats over 10 feet of reef, and disappears down another chute. It's exactly the type of skiing I'd hoped to see, and the judges rank him in the top five for the day. (I rank him first; he skied the hardest line, and he isn't even competing. He's a 19-year-old Alyeska ski patroller named Jake Young, who fore-ran the course for the hell of it.)

The women go first, with the sun popping in and out of the high clouds. Swiss phenom Francine Moreillon, who stunt-skied in the Bond flick *The World Is Not Enough,* cleans up as usual. Between heats, I spot Chris Davenport scouting his line. We chat for a few minutes and then he skis off to catch the next tram, 800 feet below. I take off after him. Accelerating fast, snow spills over his shoulders as he flows through rolling terrain before cresting a knoll and disappearing. It's just a little patch of powder, nothing extreme, but I know he's enjoying it as much as I am. Davenport heads up for his last run; I hold up at the judge's stand and wait. He ends up skiing a line very similar to Young's, sticking moderate air, blasting through small trees at the bottom. He rips—and wins.

Given his passion for freeskiing, it strikes me as odd that a skier of Davenport's caliber bothers competing. When I ask him why he shows up, he gives me the standard "I'm still at the top of my game" jock reply. But then he says something else: "It's all about soul-skiing and being out on the hill with your friends. You get that overwhelming feeling of positive energy. It's buzzing all around you."

The words remind me of something Jeff Holden, the sensei of sick-bird air, told me. "Skiing gives us the ability to be in many flows and times in the present," he said. "I've felt magic. It's filled me with faith to rid me of fear and connect with my spirit." Sure, talk like that hugs your inner bunny. But later, when I'm wondering if I'll ever get another chance to ski waist-deep Alaskan powder with a posse of whooping and hollering die-hards, I realize that not even Davenport or Holden can explain what a freeskier does—they can only do it.

# The Iceman Cometh

## Michael Finkel

*Michael Finkel is a contributing editor at* Bicycling *magazine, from which this piece comes, and is a staff writer for* Sports Illustrated.

It's February. It's icy. It's time to ride. Got a problem with that? There's a fine line between excitement and idiocy, and I have just crossed it. I'm on the idiocy side. I'm also on my mountain bike. It is mid-February, at dusk, in Vermont. Exactly zero birds are chirping. Why should they? It is so cold out that each breath forms a circle in front of me like smoke rings from a cigar. My water bottle has become a bomb-shaped block of ice. The sky is gray.

In addition to a layer of polypropylene and a full ski outfit, I'm wearing a thick ragg-wool ski cap, which I've been unable to cram beneath my helmet. What I've done is sort of balance my bike helmet atop my hat. Clearly, bicycle helmets were not designed with winter in mind. It dawns on me that perhaps there is a reason for this.

I'm moving at about 2 mph, maybe slower. The trail, which leads to the top of Rattlesnake Mountain near the tidy hamlet of Brattleboro, is steep. Very steep—you might as well round it up and call it vertical. Under normal conditions, steep isn't that big a deal. Sure, I'll bitch with the best of them, but I can get up steep. Under normal conditions.

This, however, isn't in the same hemisphere as normal. The last three days have seen a disturbing pattern of torrential rains followed by subfreezing weather followed by more rains followed by frigid cold. It's been the type of week where if you tap your car's brakes at the wrong spot you do a swift 720 [degrees] then take out the guardrail. Every five minutes some guy gets on the radio and says you shouldn't leave your home unless it's a dire emergency.

So I've gone bicycling. The Rattlesnake Mountain trail looks as though it could be ascended only by a team of mountaineers. Ice is everywhere, steel blue and frozen midwinter thick. A foot below the icy surface I can see last fall's leaves, captured in full color as if encased in glass. I am riding my regular mountain bike, with one essential alteration—each of my tires is studded with 364 small, sharp sheet-metal screws drilled through the tire from the inside. My tires look like something punk rockers might use as hula hoops.

This is all Dave King's fault. Dave is the founder of the Mount Snow Mountain Bike Center—the nation's first mountain-bike school—and a pioneer ice cyclist. He's the most passionate cyclist I have ever met. He's also a friend of mine, which is how I let him talk me into my virgin ice ride. Dave lives for weather like this—such is his fanaticism for ice that friends have nicknamed him Klondike, after the frigid region of Canada's Yukon Territory. "There are a lot of people who have no idea what my real name is," he says. "People look me up in the phone book under 'K.'" Klondike is an Abominable Snowman–sized cyclist: 13EEE shoes; 215 pounds on his six-foot frame, half of it, seemingly, on his muscle-corded thighs. "Ice," he says in a long exhale, a tone one usually reserves for addressing a lover, "is an untapped and unappreciated resource."

Dave has been riding on ice since 1987, when there were probably no more than a dozen ice cyclists in the nation. Now there are thousands, with clusters of riders in northern New England, central Colorado, and western Montana. There's a handful of organized ice races, an official club—the Alpine Snow Bicycle Association, based in Denver—and several studded-tire manufacturers. The sport is even scheduled to be included in ESPN's X Games and featured on MTV Sports. But hipness, if that's what ESPN and MTV connote, doesn't seem to jibe with the prevailing ice-cycling ethos—the few dedicated ice cyclists I've met all tend to be shy creatures, avoiding any club that would have them as a member and passing up premade wheels in favor of scrupulously constructing their own studded tires. They like to ride in small groups, on logging roads, mountain paths, or alpine lakes, on days when all but the irrational remain inside.

It's like that today, just me and Dave and Rattlesnake Mountain. We're an hour into our ride, not far from the top, on the most precipitous stretch of the trail. The ice here has solidified into overlapping layers, like a multitiered waterfall, spiderwebbed with cracks. I am no longer cold. In fact, I'm sweating as if it's August. Dave leads the way, his tires gripping solidly on the ice, each rotation producing a ripping sound like Velcro strips being pulled apart. The feat seems impossible, an illusion of sorts, as if someone were strolling casually across the ceiling. But I'm doing it. I'm cycling up a trail that looks like a luge run, and the traction feels better than rubber on dirt. I'm defying several fundamental laws of physics. I'm gritting my teeth and forcing my crank arms around and sticking to unstickable glare ice.

And then, just like that, I'm not. My tumble starts so innocuously it's almost a joke. No drama, no cataclysmic event, no sensational endo. As we're pushing up the pitch I get a little tired and then a little more tired and then so tired my legs feel like there are about two dozen cattle prods zapping against them. I begin to lose momentum. So I simply put my foot down.

Something happens to the world. One instant the scenery is plodding past in slow motion; the next it's in fast forward. Or rather fast reverse. I'm not moving uphill anymore—I'm going down. Fast. On my back. The trees are no longer trees; they're green bands of blur. The clouds have become contrails. I'm a human hockey puck, sliding and spinning down Rattlesnake Mountain.

I fly off the trail and into the woods. Around me there is much snapping and shattering. I jolt to a stop. Everything gets eerily quiet. I lie there, cradled in the woods, and take a full-body inventory. How many bones have I broken? One limb at a time, I wiggle everything. Everything wiggles. Amazing.

I grab hold of a low-lying branch and haul myself up. I see that I've put healthy gashes in both legs of my ski pants and in one elbow of my jacket. I take off a glove, put my hand inside the collar of my shirt, and press it against my right shoulder blade. My fingertips come away sticky with blood. Not terrible. I crawl on hands and knees back to the trail to retrieve my bike, which had careened most of the way with me. Nothing broken there, either. I squeeze the brakes and, using my bike as a giant crampon, I walk gingerly up the hill.

Dave is sitting on his bike at the crest, holding on to a tree trunk. "I forgot to tell you," he says. "You're not supposed to put your foot down."

He laughs. I don't.

Within five minutes we're at the summit of Rattlesnake Mountain. Vermont looks cold. I follow the rim line up and down the dome-shaped mountains.

Tendrils of chalk-white smoke curl up from brick smokestacks far below. Everything seems brittle. We don't stay long. I give my jaw a workout on a piece of rock-solid PowerBar. I suck on an icicle. Our sweat chills us and we start shivering. So we swing our bikes around and point them back down; me first, Dave following in case he needs to pick up the pieces.

I hang my butt out over my rear tire and pinch the seat between my thighs. I pull on my brake levers as hard as my frozen fingers will allow. Which isn't hard enough. The iced rims slip easily between the pads. My bike bolts down the mountain. The ice pops and cracks beneath my wheels. I battle my way around each switchback, working the fall line, trusting my bike's gyroscopic stability. I do not want to tumble again. A high-speed ice-cycling crash, I imagine, would be similar to diving headfirst into an empty swimming pool.

I ride on. My concentration sharpens and adrenaline kicks in and the speed and the absurdity and the danger and the thrill all swirl together in my head and I slip into this hyperaware state—survival mode, some people call it—my reactions are keen and my senses acute. It is a rare and wondrous phenomenon. All notion of time or distance becomes markedly dimmed. It's just the here and now that counts, and I ride in this present-tense state and there is not a single fiber of my being that is not focused on cycling.

I have no clue how long it takes to return to Dave's car. All I know is that I'm alive and I haven't fallen again. The air tastes like pine and I drink it down. My hands, I notice, have cramped into bike-braking position. I don't care. Dave pulls up behind me.

"Well," he says. He looks euphoric. This is his favorite sport and Rattlesnake is one of his cherished rides. He wants me to love it, too.

"Well, what?" The sudden stability of the ground, oddly, makes me feel disoriented. I sit down.

"Well, what do you think?"

"Dammit," I answer. It's all I can think of to say. I'm panting so hard my body is enveloped in vapor.

"Dammit, what?"

"Dammit, that was stupid."

"Anything else?" he asks. Half his face has become a grin.

"Yeah," I say. His grin is contagious. "Dammit, that was fun."

# Hang Looser

## Mark Borden

*Mark Borden is a journalist who writes for various magazines, among them* Fortune, *from which this piece is taken.*

I didn't tell my mother that I was going kitesurfing in Hawaii. I'm a grown man, yet when it comes to activities that might lead to massive reconstruction of expensive orthodontic work, I tend to keep quiet.

The best way to describe kitesurfing is by imagining several extreme sports—wakeboarding, surfing, windsurfing, hang gliding—rolled into one. But there's no need for a boat, good waves, or superstrong winds: With as little as six knots blowing, you're ready to rip. Essentially, you fly a 12-foot Mylar-and-polyester kite while surfing a customized board with foot straps that lock you in—you dangle from 60-foot lines, and the wind is your power source. Think high speeds, big air, and lots of adrenaline. Think hyperfun, the kind of fun that gone awry can really hurt. Think Mountain Dew commercials.

The bartender at Milagros, a great Mexican restaurant on Maui, stops shaking my margarita when I tell him I'll be kitesurfing the next day. "A friend tried that recently," he says. "He totally smashed his face and teeth in." I force a laugh and wait for him to say something encouraging or at least a "Hang loose, bro." Instead, he asks if I'm taking the lesson on the north shore, out by Kahului Airport. (I am.) "I had another friend who used to kitesurf out there," he says gravely. "He was yanked out of the water and shredded over a barbed-wire fence. Not pretty." I pay the check and split.

On the beach with instructor John Holzhall of Action Sports Maui, I casually mention the bartender's grim tales. "Kitemares," he says with a big smile. "Don't worry, those usually only happen to people who don't take instruction."

Action Sports offers classes that range from 1-hour lessons on basic theory and safety techniques to two-week, 40-hour instructor-training courses. I had settled on the three-hour orientation covering safety, theory, and an ominous "self-rescue" procedure (involving a razor knife); it gets you into the water and familiar with the essentials of kitesurfing. There was no guarantee I'd be skimming the Pacific at 30 miles per hour, and it was unlikely that I'd blast 40-foot air like some of the pros who were already on the water.

Kitesurfing was born in the mid-1980s when two French brothers created a wing-shaped kite with an inflatable bladder that both kept the kite from collapsing and allowed it to float. The sport didn't take off until the mid-1990s, when it migrated to Maui—home to steady winds and a ready supply of adrenaline junkies looking for the new new fix. Since then the sport's popularity has grown tremendously. In the U.S. alone, kites are tugging surfers in such states as California (obviously), North Carolina, Oregon, and New York. More than 12 companies now manufacture kitesurfing boards, and at least 10 companies produce kites; sales of kites in 2000 are expected to hit 30,000. A complete setup, not including lessons, runs about $2,500. That's cheap compared with wakeboarding, steep compared with the price of a surfboard.

No doubt, a day in the surf with a kite is a total rush. Just maintaining the kite's position and keeping your body focused on standing up takes maximum coordination and concentration. If you submit to the excitement of surfing and forget about controlling the kite, it nose-dives hard into the sea, with you following. I was so close to getting it—but one day is definitely not enough. According to Holzhall at Action Sports, I was a quick study. "One more three-hour session," he said, and my wobbly he's up/he's down beginnings would evolve into long rides with the wind at my back. Unfortunately, my time in Hawaii was up, and I had to get back to the office. Fortunately, my experience was far from a failure. Stopping through L.A., I saw my mom and told her about the assignment. She was happy to see me, especially with my smile intact.

# Bodybuilding: Steve Michalik

## Paul Solotaroff

*Paul Solotaroff served on the staff of* National Sports Daily *and is the author of* Group: Six People in Search of a Life.

Half the world was in mortal terror of him. He had a sixty-inch chest, twenty-three-inch arms, and when the Anadrol and Bolasterone backed up in his bloodstream, his eyes went as red as the laser scope on an Uzi. He threw people through windows, and chased them madly down Hempstead Turnpike when they had the temerity to cut him off. And in the gym he owned in Farmingdale, the notorious Mr. America's, if he caught you looking at him while he trained, you generally woke up, bleeding, on the pavement outside. Half out of his mind on androgens and horse steroids, he had this idea that being looked at robbed him of energy, energy that he needed to leg-press two thousand pounds.

Nonetheless, one day a kid walked up to him between sets and said, "I want to be just like you, Steve Michalik. I want to be Mr. America and Mr. Universe."

"Yeah?" said Michalik in thick contempt. "How bad do you think you want it?"

"Worse than anything in the world," said the kid, a scrawny seventeen-year-old with more balls than biceps. "I can honestly say that I would die for a body like yours."

"Well, then you probably will," snorted Michalik. "Meet me down at the beach tomorrow at six A.M. sharp. And if you're like even half a minute late . . ."

The kid was there at six A.M. pronto, freezing his ass off in a raggedy hood and sweats. "What do we do first?" he asked.

"Swim," grunted Michalik, dragging him into the ocean. Twenty yards out, Michalik suddenly seized the kid by his scalp and pushed him under a wave. The kid flailed punily, wriggling like a speared eel. A half minute, maybe forty-five seconds, passed before Michalik let the kid up, sobbing out seawater. He gave the kid a breath, then shoved him down again, holding him under this time until the air bubbles stopped, whereupon he dragged him out by the hood and threw him, gasping, on the beach.

"When you want the title as bad as you wanted that last fucking breath," sneered Michalik, "then and only then can you come talk to me."

For himself, Michalik only wanted two things anymore. He wanted to walk on stage at the Beacon Theater on November 15, 1986, professional bodybuilding's Night of Champions, and just turn the joint out with his 260 pounds of ripped, stripped, and shrink-wrapped muscle. And then, God help him, he wanted to die. Right there, in front of everybody, with all the flashbulbs popping, he wanted to drop dead huge and hard at the age of thirty-nine, and leave a spectacular corpse behind.

The pain, you see, had become just unendurable. Ten years of shotgunning steroids had turned his joints into fish jelly and spiked his blood pressure so high he had to pack his nose to stop the bleeding. He'd been pissing blood for months, and what was coming out of him now was *brown,* pure protoplasm that his engorged liver hadn't the wherewithal to break down. And when he came home from the gym at night, his whole body was in spasm. His eight-year-old boy, Steve Junior, had to pack his skull in ice, trying to take the top 10 percent off his perpetual migraine.

"I knew it was all over for me," Michalik says. "Every system in my body was shot, my testicles had shrunk to the size of cocktail peanuts. It was only a question of which organ was going to explode on me first.

"See, we'd all of us [professional bodybuilders] been way over the line for years, and it was like, suddenly, all the bills were coming in. Victor Faizowitz took so much shit that his brain exploded. The Aldactazone [a diuretic] sent his body temperature up to one hundred twelve degrees, and he literally melted to death. Another guy, an Egyptian bodybuilder training for the Mr. Universe contest, went the same way, a massive hemorrhage from head to toe—died bleeding out of every orifice. And Tommy Sansone, a former Mr. America who'd been my very first mentor in the gym, blew out his immune system on Anadrol and D-ball [Dianabol], and died of tumors all over his body.

"As for me, I couldn't wait to join 'em. I had so much evil in me from all the drugs I was taking that I'd go home at night and ask God why he hadn't killed me yet. And then, in the next breath, I'd say, 'Please, I know I've done a lot of terrible things—sold steroids to kids, beaten the shit out of strangers—but please don't let me go out like a sucker, God. Please let me die hitting that last pose at the Beacon, with the crowd on its feet for a second standing O.'"

Michalik's prayers might better have been addressed to a liver specialist. Two weeks before the show, he woke up the house at four in the morning with an excruciating pain beneath his rib cage. His wife, Thomasina, long since practiced at such emergencies, ran off to fetch some ice.

"Fuck the ice," he groaned. "Call Dr. Ludwig."

Dr. Arthur Ludwig, a prominent endocrinologist who had been treating Michalik on and off for a number of years, was saddened but unsurprised by the call. "Frankly," he told Michalik, "I've been expecting it now for ages. Your friends have been telling me lately how bad you've been abusing the stuff, especially for the last five years."

That he certainly had. Instead of cycling on and off steroids, giving his body here and there a couple months' recuperation, Michalik had been juicing pretty much constantly since 1976, shooting himself with fourteen different drugs and swallowing copious amounts of six or seven others. Then there was all the speed he was gulping— bennies, black beauties—to get through his seven-hour workouts, and the handful of downs at night to catch four hours of tortuous sleep.

There, at any rate, Michalik was, doubled over in bed at four in the morning, his right side screaming like a bomb had gone off in it.

"You'd better get him to New York Hospital as fast as you can," Ludwig told Michalik's wife over the phone. "They've got the best liver specialist on the East Coast there. I'll meet you in his office in an hour."

At the hospital, they pumped Michalik full of morphine and took a hasty sonogram upstairs. The liver specialist, a brusque Puritan who'd been apprised of Michalik's steroid usage, called him into his office.

"See this?" he pointed to the sonogram, scarcely concealing a sneer. "This is what's left of your liver, Mr. Michalik. And these"— indicating the four lumps grouped inside it, one of them the size of a ripe grapefruit—"these are hepatic tumors. You have advanced liver cancer, sir."

"I do?" grinned Michalik, practically hugging himself for joy. "How long you think I've got?"

"Mr. Michalik, do you understand what I'm telling you?" snapped the doctor, apparently miffed that his news hadn't elicited operatic grief. "You have cancer, and will be dead within weeks or days if I don't operate immediately. And frankly, your chances of surviving surgery are—"

"Surgery!" blurted Michalik, looking at the man as if he were bonkers. "You're not coming near me with a knife. That would leave a *scar.*"

The doctor was with perfect justice about to order Michalik out of his office when Ludwig walked in. He took a long look at the sonogram and announced that surgery was out of the question. Michalik's liver was so compromised, he would undoubtedly die on the table. Besides, Ludwig adjudged, those weren't tumors at all. They were something rarer by far but no less deadly: steroid-induced cysts, or thick sacs of blood and muscle, that were full to bursting— and growing.

He ordered Michalik strapped down—the least movement now could perforate the cysts—and wheeled upstairs to intensive care. The next twenty-four hours, he declared, would tell the tale. If, deprived of steroids, the cysts stopped growing, there was a small chance that Michalik might come out of this. If, on the other hand, they fed on whatever junk he'd injected the last couple of days—well, he'd get his wish, at any rate, to die huge.

Michalik knew it was the liver, of course. He might have been heedless, but he was hardly uninformed. In fact, he knew so much about steroids that he'd written a manual on their use, and gone on the *Today* show to debate doctors about their efficacy. Like the steroid gurus of southern California, Michalik was a self-taught sorcerer whose laboratory was his body. From the age of eleven, he'd read voraciously in biochemistry, obsessed about finding out what made people big. He walked the streets of Brooklyn as a teenager, knocking on physicians' doors, begging to be made enlightened

about protein synthesis. And years later he scoured the *Physicians'
Desk Reference* from cover to cover, searching not for steroids but for
other classes of drugs whose secondary function was to grow muscle.

Steroids, Michalik knew, were a kind of God's play, a way of
rewriting his own DNA. He'd grown up skinny and hating himself
to his very cell level. According to Michalik, his father, a despotic
drunk with enormous forearms, beat him with whatever was close to
hand, and smashed his face, for fun, into a plate of mashed potatoes.

"I was small and weak, and my brother Anthony was big and
graceful, and my old man made no bones about loving him and hating me," Michalik recalls. "The minute I walked in from school, it
was, 'You worthless little shit, what are you doing home so early?'
His favorite way to torture me was to tell me he was going to put me
in a *home*. We'd be driving along in Brooklyn somewhere, and we'd
pass a building with iron bars on the windows, and he'd stop the car
and say to me, 'Get out. This is the home we're putting you in.' I'd be
standing there, sobbing on the curb—I was maybe eight or nine at
the time—and after a while he'd let me get back into the car and
drive off laughing at his little joke."

Fearful and friendless throughout childhood—even his
brother was leery of being seen with him—Michalik hid out in comic
books and Steve Reeves movies, burning to become huge and invul-
nerable. At thirteen, he scrubbed toilets in a Vic Tanny spa just to be
in the presence of that first generation of iron giants—Eddie Juliani
and Leroy Colbert, among others. At twenty, stationed at an air
force base in Southeast Asia, he ignored sniper fire and the 120-
degree heat to bench-press a cinder-block barbell in an open clearing,
telling the corps psychiatrist that he couldn't be killed because it was
his destiny to become Mr. America. And at thirty-four, years after
he'd forgotten where he put all his trophies, he was still crawling out
of bed at two in the morning to eat his eighth meal of the day because
he *still* wasn't big enough. As always, there was that fugitive inch or

two missing, that final heft without which he wouldn't even take his shirt off on the beach—for fear that everyone would laugh.

And so, of course, there were steroids. They'd been around since at least the mid-1930s, when Hitler had them administered to his SS thugs to spike their bloodlust. By the 1950s, the eastern bloc nations were feeding them to schoolkids, creating a generation of bioengineered athletes. And in the late 1960s, anabolics hit the beaches of California, as U.S. drug companies discovered that there was a vast new market out there of kids who'd swallow anything to double their pecs and their pleasure.

The dynamics of anabolic steroids have been pretty well understood for years. Synthetic variations of the male hormone testosterone, they enter the bloodstream as chemical messengers and attach themselves to muscle cells. Once attached to these cells, they deliver their twofold message: grow, and increase endurance.

Steroids accomplish the first task by increasing the synthesis of protein. In sufficient quantities, they turn the body into a kind of fusion engine, converting everything, including fat, into mass and energy. A chemical bodybuilder can put on fifty pounds of muscle in six months because most of the six thousand to ten thousand calories he eats a day are incorporated, not excreted.

The second task—increasing endurance—is achieved by stimulating the synthesis of a molecule called creatine phosphate, or CP. CP is essentially hydraulic fluid for muscles, allowing them to do more than just a few seconds' work. The more CP you have in your tank, the more power you generate. Olympic weightlifters and defensive linemen have huge stockpiles of CP, some portion of which is undoubtedly genetic. The better part of it, though, probably comes out of a bottle of Anadrol, a popular oral steroid that makes you big, strong, and savage—and not necessarily in that order.

Over the course of eleven years, Michalik had taken ungodly amounts of Anadrol. If his buddies were taking two 50 mg tablets a day, he took four. Six weeks later, when he started to plateau, he jacked the ante to eight. So, too, with Dianabol, another brutal oral steroid. Where once a single 5 mg pill sufficed, inevitably he was gulping ten or twelve of them a day, in conjunction with the Anadrol.

The obstacle here was his immune system, which was stubbornly going on about its business, neutralizing these poisons with antibodies and shutting down receptor sites on the muscle cells. No matter. Michalik, upping the dosage, simply overwhelmed his immune system, and further addled it by flooding his bloodstream with other drugs.

All the while, of course, he was cognizant of the damage done. He knew, for instance, that Anadrol, like all oral steroids, was utter hell on the liver. An alkylated molecule with a short carbon chain, it had to be hydralized, or broken down, within twenty-four hours. This put enormous stress on his liver, which had thousands of other chemical transactions to carry out every day, not the least of which was processing the waste from his fifty pounds of new muscle. The *Physicians' Desk Reference* cautions that the smallest amounts of Anadrol may be toxic to the liver, even in patients taking it for only a couple of months for anemia:

> *Warning:* May cause peliosis hepatis, a condition in which liver tissue is replaced with blood-filled cysts, often causing liver failure. . . . Often not recognized until life-threatening liver failure or intra-abdominal hemorrhage occurs. . . . Fatal malignant liver tumors are also reported.

As lethal as it was, however, Anadrol was like a baby food compared to some of the other stuff Michalik was taking. On the bodybuilding black market, where extraordinary things are still available, Michalik and some of his buddies bought the skulls of dead monkeys. Cracking them open with their bare hands, they drank the hormone-rich fluid that poured out of the hypothalamus gland. They filled enormous syringes with a French supplement called Triacana and, aiming for the elusive thyroid gland, *shot it right into their necks.* They took so much Ritalin before workouts to psych themselves up that one of Michalik's training partners, a former Mr. Eastern USA, ran out of the gym convinced that he could stop a car with his bare hands. He stood in the passing lane of the Hempstead Turnpike, his feet spread shoulder-width apart, bracing for the moment of impact—and got run over like a dog by a Buick Skylark, both his legs and arms badly broken.

Why, knowing what he knew about these poisons, did Michalik continue taking them? Because he, as well as his buddies and so many thousands of other bodybuilders and football players, were fiercely and progressively addicted to steroids. The American medical community is currently divided about whether or not the stuff is addictive. These are the same people who declared, after years of thorough study, that *steroids do not grow muscle.* Bodybuilders are still splitting their sides over that howler. Michalik, however, is unamused.

"First, those morons at the AMA say that steroids don't work, which anyone who's ever been inside a gym knows is bullshit," he snorts. "Then, ten years later, they tell us they're deadly. Oh, now they're deadly? Shit, that was like the FDA seal of approval for steroids. C'mon, everybody, they *must* be good for you—the AMA says they'll kill you!

"Somehow, I don't know how, I escaped getting addicted to them the first time, when I was training for the Mr. America in 1972. Maybe it was because I was on them for such a short stretch, and went relatively light on the stuff. Mostly, all it amounted to was a shot in the ass once a week from a doctor in Roslyn. I never found out what was in that shot, but Jesus, did it make me crazy. Here I was, a churchgoing, gentle Catholic, and suddenly I was pulling people out of restaurant booths and threatening to kill them just because there were no other tables open. I picked up a three-hundred-pound railroad tie and caved in the side of some guy's truck with it because I thought he'd insulted my wife. I was a nut, a psycho, constantly out of control—and then, thank God, the contest came, and I won it and got off the juice, and suddenly became human again. I retired, and devoted myself entirely to my wife for all the hell I'd put her through, and swore I'd never go near that shit again."

A couple of years later, however, something happened that sent him back to the juice, and this time there was no getting off it. "I'd bought Thomasina a big house in Farmingdale, and filled it with beautiful things, and was happier than I'd ever been in my life. And then one day I found out she'd been having an affair. I was worse than wiped out, my soul was ripped open. It had taken me all those years to finally feel like I was a man, to get over all the things my father had done to me . . . and she cut my fucking heart out."

Michalik went back to the gym, where he'd always solved all his problems, and started seeing someone we'll call Dr. X. A physician and insider in the subculture, for two decades Dr. X had been supplying bodybuilders with all manner of steroids in exchange for sexual favors. Michalik hit him up for a stack of prescriptions, but made it clear that he couldn't accommodate the doctor sexually, to the latter's keen disappointment. The two, however, worked out a satisfactory compromise. Michalik, the champion bodybuilder who was constantly being consulted by young wannabes, directed some of them posthaste to the tender governance of Dr. X.

"They had to find out sooner or later that the road to the title went through Dr. X's office," Michalik shrugs. "Nobody on this coast was gonna get to be competition size unless they put out for him— that, or they had a daddy in the pharmaceutical business. The night Dr. X first tried to seduce me, he showed me pictures of five different champions that he said he'd had sex with. I checked it out later and found out it was all true. Nice business, isn't it, professional bodybuilding? More pimps and whores than Hollywood."

Michalik didn't care about any of that, however. Nor did he care if he went crazy or got addicted to steroids. "I didn't care if I fucking died from 'em. All I cared about was getting my body back. I was down to one hundred fifty pounds, which was my natural body weight, and no one in the gym even knew who I was. Big guys were screaming at me, 'Get off that bench, you little punk, I wanna use it!' Three months later, I'm two hundred pounds and bench-pressing four hundred, and the same guys are coming over to me, going, 'Hey, aren't you Steve Michalik? When did you get here?' And I'd tell 'em, 'I've been here for the last three months, motherfucker. I'm the guy you pushed offa that bench over there, remember?'"

By that third month, he recalls, he was hopelessly hooked on steroids, unable to leave the house without "gulping three of something, and taking a shot of something else. I'd get out of bed in the morning feeling weak and sick, and stagger around, going 'Where's my shit?' I was a junkie and I knew it and I hated myself for it. But what I hated much, much more was not getting to Dr. X's office. He had the *real* hot shit—Primobolan, Parabolin—that you couldn't get anywhere else. They were so powerful you felt them *immediately* in your muscles, and tasted them for hours on your lips. My heart would start pounding, and the blood would come pouring out of my nose, but he'd just pack it with cotton and send me on my way.

"Suddenly, all I was doing was living and dying for those shots. I was totally obsessed about seeing him, I'd have terrible panic attacks on the subway, my brain would be racing—was I going to make it up to his office before I fell down? I was throwing people out of my way, shoving 'em into poles, practically knocking the door down before we pulled into the station.

"Understand, there was no justification for the things I did; not my wife's affair, not what had happened to me as a kid—nothing. I was an adult, I knew what I was doing, at least at the beginning, and when you add it all up, I deserve to have died from it.

"But I want you to understand what it's like to just completely lose yourself. To get buried in something so deep that you think the only way out is to die. Those ten years, it was like I was trapped inside a robot body, watching myself do horrible things, and yelling, 'Stop! Stop!' but I couldn't even slow down. It was always *more* drugs, and *more* side effects, and *more* drugs for the side effects. For ten years, I was just an animal on stimulus-response."

He flew to London in the fall of 1975 for the Mr. Universe show, already so sick from the steroids and the eight meals a day that he could scarcely make it up the stairs to the stage. "I had a cholesterol level of over four hundred, my blood pressure was two-forty over one-ten—but, Jesus Christ, I was a great-looking corpse. No one had ever seen anything like me on stage before, I had absolutely *perfect* symmetry: nineteen-inch arms, nineteen-inch calves, and a fifty-four-inch chest that was exactly twice the size of my thighs. The crowd went bazongo, the judges all loved me—and none of it, not even the title, meant shit to me. Joy, pride, any sense of satisfaction—the drugs wiped all of that out of me. The only feeling I was capable of anymore was deep, deep hatred."

Michalik went home, threw his trophy into a closet, and began training maniacally for the Mr. Olympia show, bodybuilding's most prestigious event. He'd invented a training regimen called "Intensity/Insanity," which called for *seventy* sets per body part instead of the customary ten. This entailed a seven-hour workout and excruciating pain, but the steroids, he found, turned that pain into pleasure, "a huge release of all the pressure built up inside me, the rage and the energy."

And with whatever rage and energy he had left, he ran his wife's panicked lover out of town, and completed his revenge by impregnating her "so that there'd be *two* Steve Michaliks in the world to oppress her." Spotlessly faithful to her for the first ten years of their marriage, he began nailing everyone he could get his hands on now, thanks in no small part to his daily dosage of Halotestin, a steroid whose chief side effect was a constant—and conspicuous— erection. He was also throwing down great heaps of Clomid and HCG, two fertility drugs for women that, in men, stimulate the production of testosterone.

"Bottom line, I was insatiable, and acting it out all over the place. I had girlfriends in five different towns in Long Island, and one day I was so hormone-crazed I fucked 'em all, one right after the other. Suddenly, I saw why there was so much rampant sex in this business, why the elite bodybuilders always had two or three girls in their hotel room, or were making thousands of dollars a weekend at private gay parties. In fact, one of my friends in the business, a former Mr. America, used to get so horny on tour that he'd fuck the Coke machine in his hotel. Swear to God, he'd stick his dick in the change slot and bang it for all he was worth. I'm telling you, my wife saw him do this, she can vouch for it. He fucked those machines from coast to coast, and even had ratings for them. I seem to remember the Chicago Hyatt's being pretty high up there on the list."

Hot, in any event, off his win in the Mr. Universe, and absolutely galactic now at 250 pounds, he was the consensus pick among his peers to put an end to Arnold Schwarzenegger's reign as Mr. Olympia and begin a five- or six-year run of his own. He had even prepped himself to follow Arnold into show business, taking two years of acting lessons and a year of speech at Weiss-Baron Studios in Manhattan. One of the networks approached him about hosting a science show. George Butler and Charles Gaines filmed him extensively for *Pumping Iron,* the definitive bodybuilding flick that put Schwarzenegger on the map in Hollywood.

And then, driving himself to the airport for the Mr. Olympia show that November, Michalik suddenly ran into something bigger than steroids. A tractor-trailer driver, neglecting to check his mirror, veered into Michalik's lane on Route 109 and ran right over the hood of his Mustang. Michalik was dragged twenty yards into an embankment; the Mustang crumpled up around him. When they finally sawed him out of it two hours later, he had four cracked discs and a torn sciatic nerve, and was completely paralyzed from the waist down.

The bad news, said the surgeon after a battery of X rays, was that Michalik would never walk again. The good news was that with a couple of operations, the pain could be substantially mitigated. Michalik told him to get the fuck out of his room. For months he lay in traction, refusing medication, and with his free arm went on injecting himself with testosterone, which he'd had with him in a black bag at the time of the accident, and which the hospital had so thoughtfully put on his bedside table.

"It was hilarious. The idiot doctors kept coming in and going, 'Gee, your blood pressure seems awfully high, Mr. Michalik,' and I'd just lie there with a straight face and go, 'Well, I *have* been very tense, you know, since the accident.'

"Meanwhile, for the one and only time in my life, the steroids were actually helping me. They speeded up the healing, which is actually their medical purpose, and kept enough size on me so that the nurses used to fight over who was supposed to wash me every day. I started getting a little sensation back in my right leg, enough so that when the doctor told me he'd send me home if I could stand up, I managed to fake it by standing on one leg."

There, however, the progress halted, and Michalik, unspeakably depressed, lay in bed for a year, bloating on steroids and chocolate chip cookies. He got a call from the TV people, telling him that they'd hired Leonard Nimoy to replace him on the science show. He got another one from the producers of *Pumping Iron,* informing him that he'd been all but cut out of the film. Worst of all, his friends and training partners jumped ship on him, neither calling nor coming by to see him.

"So typical of bodybuilders," he sneers. "'Hey, Michalik's crippled, I gotta go see him—nah, it's Tuesday, chest-and-back day. Fuck him.' But the *real* reason, I think, was they couldn't stand to see one of their own hurt. In order to keep on doing what they're doing—the drugs, the binge eating, the sex-for-money—they've gotta keep lying to themselves, saying, 'I can't be hurt, I can't get sick. I'm Superman. Cancer is *afraid* to live in my body.'"

About the only person who didn't abandon him was his kid brother, Paulie, an adopted eight-year-old who utterly worshipped Michalik. "He used to come into my room every day and massage my legs, going, 'You feel anything yet? You feel it?' He's stubborn like me. He just refused to give up, he kept saying, 'You're a *champion,* Steve, you're my hero, you're gonna be back.'

"And then one day we're watching TV, and a pro body-building show comes on. This was 1978, and the networks had started up a Grand Prix tour to cash in on the fad after *Pumping Iron.* I'm watching all the guys and just going crazy, wishing I could just get up on stage against 'em one more time, and Paulie goes, 'You *can* do it, Steve. You can come back and whip those guys. I'll help you in the gym.'"

Aroused, Michalik called an old friend, Julie Levine, and begged him for the keys to his new gym in Amityville. The next night, he got out of bed at two A.M. and scuttled to the window, where Paulie assisted him over the sash. Crawling across the lawn to his wife's car, Michalik got in the driver's seat and pushed his dead legs back, making room for his little brother beneath the steering wheel. As he steered, Paulie worked the gas and brake pedals with his hands, and in this manner they accomplished the ten miles to Amityville.

In the gym, Paulie dragged him from machine to machine, helping him push the weight stacks up. Michalik's upper body responded quickly—muscle has remarkable memory—but his legs, particularly the left one, lay there limp as old celery. After several months, however, the pain started up in them. Sharp and searing, it was as if someone had stuck a fork in his sciatic nerve. Michalik, a self-made master of pain, couldn't have been happier if he'd hit the lottery.

"The doctors all told me it would be ten years, if ever, for the nerve to come back, and here it was howling like a monster. I kicked up the dosages of all the stuff I was taking, and started *attacking* the weights instead of just lifting 'em. Six months later, the pain was so bad I still could barely straighten up—but I was leg-pressing seven hundred and eight hundred pounds, and my thighs were as big as a bear's."

And a year after that, he walked on stage in Florida, an unadvertised guest poser at the end of a Grand Prix show. The crowd, recognizing a miracle when it saw one, went berserk as Michalik modeled those thirty-four-inch thighs, each of which was considerably wider than his twenty-seven-inch waist. Schwarzenegger, in the broadcast booth doing color for ABC, was overwhelmed. "I don't believe what I am seeing," he gasped. "It's Steve Michalik, the phantom bodybuilder!"

There Michalik should have left it. He was alive, and ambulatory, and his cult status was set. Thanks to Arnie, he would be forever known as the Phantom Bodybuilder, a tag he could have turned into a merchandising gold mine, and retired.

But like a lot of other steroid casualties, Michalik couldn't stop pushing his luck. He had to keep going, had to keep *growing,* testing the limits of his skeleton and the lining of his liver. If he'd gotten galactic, he figured, on last year's drugs, there was no telling how big he could get on this year's crop. A new line of killer juice was coming out of southern California—Hexalone, Bolasterone, Dehydralone—preposterously toxic compounds that sent the liver into warp drive but which grew hard, mature muscle right before your very eyes. Sexier still, there was that new darling of the pro circuit, human growth hormone, and who knew where the ceiling even *began* on that stuff?

Instead of pulling over, then, Michalik put the hammer down. He joined the Grand Prix tour immediately after the show in Florida and began the brutal grind of doing twelve shows annually. Before the tour, top bodybuilders did five shows a year, tops—the Mr. Olympia, the Night of Champions, and two or three others in Europe—which gave them several months to recuperate from the drugs and heavy training. Now, thanks to TV, they had to do a show a month. The pace was quite literally murderous.

"Not only did guys have to peak every month, they had to keep getting *better* as the year went on. No downtime, no rest from the bingeing and fasting—you could see guys turning green from all the shit in their systems. As you might expect, some of them were falling by the wayside, one guy from arrhythmia, another guy from heart attacks.

"As for me, all I knew was that I was spending every dime I had on drugs. It cost me twenty-five thousand dollars that first year just to keep up, and that was *without* human growth hormone, which I couldn't even afford. The sport had become like an arms race now. If you heard that some guy was using Finajet, then *you* had to have it, no matter what it cost or where you had to go to get it. It actually paid to fly back and forth to France every couple of months, where you could buy the crap off the shelves of some country pharmacy and save yourself thousands of bucks.

"Needless to say, those five years on the tour were the most whacked-out of my life. My cognitive mind went on like a permanent stroll, and I became an enormous, lethal caveman. The only reason I didn't spend most of that time in jail was because two-thirds of the cops in town were customers of mine. They belonged to my gym, and bought their steroids from me, and when I got into a little beef, which was practically every other day, they took care of it on the QT for me.

"Once I was on Hempstead Turnpike, on my way to the gym, when some guy in a pickup gave me the finger. That's it, lights out. I chased him doing ninety in my new Corvette, and did a three-sixty in heavy traffic right in front of him. I jumped out, ripped the door off his truck, and caved in his face with one punch. The other guy in the cab, who had done nothing to me, jumps out and starts running down the divider to get away from me. I chased him on foot and was pounding the shit out of him on the side of the road when the cops pulled up in two cruisers. 'Michalik, get outta here, ya crazy fuck,' they go, 'this is the last goddamn time we're lettin' you slide.'"

Word quickly got around town that Michalik was to be avoided at all costs. That went double for the wild-style gym he opened, which did everything but hang a sign out saying, STEROIDS FOR SALE HERE. There were plaques on the walls that proclaimed, UP THE DOSAGE! and pictures not of stars but of twenty-gauge syringes.

As for the clientele, it ran heavily toward the highly crazed. There was the seven-foot juice freak who stomped around muttering, "I'll kill you all. I'll rip your guts out and eat them right there." There was the mob hit man who drove up in a limo every day and checked his automatic weapons at the door. There was the herpetologist who came in with a python wrapped around him, trailing a huge sea turtle, for good measure, on a leash. There was the former Mr. America who was so distraught when his dog died that he had it stuffed, and dragged it around the gym from station to station.

"I had every freak and psycho within a three-hundred-mile radius," Michalik recalls. "At night, there'd be all these animals hanging around outside my gym, slurping protein shakes and twirling biker chains—and every single one of 'em was afraid of me. That was the only way I kept 'em in line. As crazy as they all were, they knew I was crazier, and that I'd just as soon kill 'em as re-enroll 'em."

If that sounds like dubious business practice, consider that a year after opening, Michalik was so successful that he had to move to a location twice the size. But for all the money he was making, and for all the scams he was running—selling "Banana Packs," a worthless mixture of rotten bananas and egg powder, as his "secret muscle formula" for twenty-five dollars a pop; passing himself off as a veterinarian to get cases of human growth hormone at wholesale for his "clinical experiments"—he was still being bankrupted by his skyrocketing drug bills.

The federal heat had begun to come down on the steroid racket, closing out the pill-mill pharmacies where Michalik was filling his scrips. The national demand, moreover, for the high-octane stuff—Hexalone, Bolasterone, et cetera—was going through the roof, which meant that Michalik, like everybody else, had to get on line, and pay astronomical prices for his monthly package from Los Angeles.

Constantly broke, and going nowhere fast on the Grand Prix tour—"where in the beginning I'd been finishing third or fourth in the shows, by 1983 I was coming in like eleventh or twelfth"—Michalik began caving in emotionally and physically. He'd come home from the gym at night, dead-limbed and nauseous, and suddenly burst into tears without warning. Cut off from everyone, even the stouthearted Thomasina, who had finally thrown up her hands and stopped caring what he did to himself, he sat alone in a dark room, hearing his joints jowl, and dreamed about killing himself.

"I was just lost, gone, in a constant state of male PMS—the hormones flying around inside, my mood going yoyo. I just wanted an end to it; an end to all the pain I was in, and to the pain I was causing others.

"I mean, of course I had tried to get off the drugs, and always it just got worse. The depression got deeper, the craving was incredible, and those last couple of years, I was worse than any crackhead. As crazed as I was, I'd've killed to keep going, to get my hands on that next shipment of Deca or Maxibolin."

As for his body, it was finally capitulating to all the accumulated toxins. By 1983, he was bleeding from everywhere: his gums, kidneys, colon, and sinuses. The headaches started up, so piercing and obdurate that he developed separate addictions to Percodan and Demerol. And worst of all (by Michalik's lights), his muscles suddenly went soft on him. No matter how he worked them or what he shot into them, they lost their gleaming, osmotic hardness, and began to pooch out like twenty-dollar whitewalls.

His last two years on the tour were a run-on nightmare. He almost dropped dead at a show in Toronto, collapsing on stage in head-to-toe convulsions; the promoters, disgraced, hauled him off by the ankles. There was a desperate attempt in 1985, after his cholesterol hit five hundred, to wean himself from steroids once and for all. His testosterone level plummeted, however, his sperm count went to zero, and all the estrogen in his body, which had been accruing for years, turned his pecs into soft, doughy breasts. Such friends as he still had pointed out that his ass was plumping like a woman's, and tweaked him for his sexy new hip-swishing walk.

He ran to one endocrinologist after another, begging them for something to reverse the condition. To a man, each pointed to Michalik's liver reading and showed him out of his office. Leaving, he had the distinct feeling that they were laughing at him.

And so, after weighing his options—a bleak, emasculated life off steroids or a slam-bang, macho death on them—Michalik emphatically chose the latter. He packed a bag, grabbed his weight belt, and caught a plane for L.A., winding up for nine months in the valley, where all the chemical studs were training.

Just up the freeway, a cartel of former med students were minting drugs so new they scarcely had names for them yet. The stuff ran $250, $300 a bottle, but pumped you up like an air hose and kept you that way. It also made you violently sick to your stomach, but Michalik didn't have time to worry about that. He simply ran to the bathroom to heave up his guts, then came back and ripped off another thirty sets.

His hair fell out in heavy clumps; a dry cough emanated from his liver, wracking him. Every joint was inflamed; it was excruciating even to walk now. But at night, in bed and in too much pain to sleep, it cheered him to think that he would finally be dead soon, and that it would take eight men to carry his casket.

He came back to New York in the fall of 1986, on his last legs but enormous and golden brown. All along, he'd targeted the Night of Champions, to be held that November at the Beacon Theater, as his swan song. It was the Academy Awards show of bodybuilding. Everyone would be there, all the stars and cognoscenti, and it would consolidate his legend to show up one last time, coming out of a coffin to the tune of Elton John's "Funeral for a Friend." Of course, it would *really* help matters if he could drop dead on stage, but that seemed too much to hope for. All that mattered, finally, was that he go out with twenty-five hundred people thundering their approval, drowning out, once and for all, his old man's malediction that he'd never amount to shit.

And then, two weeks before the show, he woke up at four in the morning with his liver on fire, and that was the end of all that.

Happily afloat on morphine and Nembutol, Michalik drifted for seventy-two hours, dreaming that he was dead. In the course of those three days, however, his extraordinary luck held up. The huge cysts in his liver stabilized and began to shrink, though they'd so eviscerated the organ already that there was practically nothing left of it. Short of a transplant, it would be months before he could so much as sit up and take nourishment. His bodybuilding career, in any case, was finished.

When Michalik awoke in intensive care, he was inconsolable. Not only was he still unaccountably alive, his beautiful body was dissolving and going away from him. His muscles, bereft of steroids and the five pounds of chicken he ate a day, decomposed and flowed into his bloodstream as waste. In three weeks, he lost more than 100 pounds, literally pissing himself down to 147 from a steady weight of 255.

Predictably, his kidneys began to fail, functioning at 60 percent, then 40, then 20. His black hair turned gray, and the skin hung off him in folds. His father came in and told him, with all his customary tact, that he looked like an eighty-five-year-old man.

In the few hours a day that he was lucid, Michalik wept uncontrollably. Out of the unlikeliest materials—bad genes, a small bone structure, and a thoroughly degraded ego—he had assembled this utterly remarkable thing, a body that no less than Arnold Schwarzenegger once venerated as the very best in the world. Now he was too weak to lift his head off the pillow. He lay there inert for months and months, the very image, it seemed to him, of his old man's foretelling.

"I was just like Lyle Alzado, who I went to high school in Brooklyn with: weak and broken-down, leaning on my wife to keep me alive. She came and fed me every day through a straw, and swiped the huge bunch of pills I was saving to kill myself. To thank her for still being there after everything, I sold the gym and gave her all the money from it. I didn't want any of it, I didn't want anything. I just wanted to lie in bed and be miserable by myself. I was so depressed I could hardly move my jaws to speak."

Finally, by the spring of 1988, he'd recovered sufficiently to get out of bed for short stretches. Possessed by the sudden urge to atone for his sins, Michalik called every promoter he knew, begging them to let him go on stage in his condition and dramatize the wages of steroids. Surprisingly, several of them agreed to the idea. They brought Michalik out, a bag of bones in a black shirt, and let him turn the place into a graveyard for ten minutes.

"All these twenty-year-olds would be staring up at me with their jaws hanging open, and I'd get on the mike and say, 'You think this can't happen to you, tough guy? You think you know more about steroids than I do? Well, I wrote the book on 'em, buddy, and they *still* ate me up. I'm forty years old and I'm finished. Dead.'"

The former proselytizer for steroids got some grim satisfaction out of spreading the gospel against them. He dragged himself out to high schools and hard-core juice gyms, using himself as a walking cautionary tale. But whatever his good works were doing for his soul, they weren't doing a damn thing for his body. He still woke up sick in every cell, poisoned by the residue of all the drugs. The liver cysts, shrunk to the size of golf balls but no farther, sapped his strength and forced him to eat like a sparrow, subsisting on farina and chicken soup. His hormones were wildly scrambled—a blood test revealed he had the testosterone level of a twelve-year-old *girl*— and it had been two years since he'd had even a twinge of an erection. Indeed, his moods were so erratic that he had his wife commit him to a stretch in a Long Island nut bin.

"I wasn't crazy, but I didn't know what else to do. All day long I just sat there, consumed with self-hatred: 'Why did you do this? Why did you do that?' I mean, even when I was huge, I never had what you would call the greatest relationship with myself, but now it was 'You're *weak!* You're *tiny!* You're *stupid!* You're *worthless!'*— and what the hell was I going to say to shut it up? The only thing I'd ever valued about myself was my body, and I'd totally, systematically fucked it up. My life, as you can probably guess, was intolerable."

It was here, however, that fate stepped in and cut Michalik a whopping break. Halfway across the world, an Australian rugby player named Joe Reesh somehow heard about Michalik's plight and called to tell him about a powerful new detox program. It was a brutally arduous deal—an hour of running, then five hours straight in a 180-degree sauna, for a minimum of twenty-one days—but infallibly, it leached the poisons out of your fat cells, where they'd otherwise sit, crystallized, for the rest of your life.

Utterly desperate, Michalik gave it a shot. He could scarcely jog around the block that first day, but in the sauna, it all started coming out of him: a viscous, green paste that oozed out of his eyes and nostrils. By the end of the first week, he reports, he was running two miles; by the end of the second, his ex-wife verifies, his gray hair had turned black again. And when he stepped out of the sauna after the twenty-third and final day, his skin was as pink and snug as a teenager's. Liver and kidney tests confirmed the wildly improbable: He was perfectly healthy again.

"Everything came back to me: my sense of humor, my lust for life—hell, my lust, *period*. Don't forget, it'd been almost three years since I'd gotten it up—I had some serious business to take care of. But the greatest thing by far was what *wasn't* there anymore. All the biochemical hatred I'd been walking around with for twelve years, it was like that all bled out of me with the green stuff, and I had this overpowering need to be with people again, especially my son, Stevie. I had tons of making up to do with him, and I've loved every minute of it. It kills me that I could've let myself get so sick that I was ready to die and leave him."

Michalik went to his wife and told her he was going back to bodybuilding. It was his life, his art, he couldn't leave it alone—only this time, he swore on heaven, he was going to do it clean. She understood, or at least tried to, but said she couldn't go through with it again: the two A.M. feedings, the five-hundred-dollar-a-week grocery bills. They parted amicably, and Michalik returned to the gym, as zealous and single-minded as a monk. In the last two years he's put on 60 pounds, and looks dense and powerful at 225, though he's sober about the realities.

"There are *nineteen-year-olds* clocking in now at two sixty-five," he says, shaking his head. "The synthetic HGH [human growth hormone] has evolved a new species in five years. By the end of the decade, the standard will be three-hundred-pounders, with twenty-three-inch necks that are almost as big as their waists.

"But all around the country, kids'll be dropping dead from the stuff, and getting diabetes because it burns out their pancreas. I don't care what those assholes in California say, there's no such thing in the world as a 'good' drug. There's only bad drugs and sick bastards who want to sell them to you."

Someone ought to post those words in every high school in the country. The latest estimate from a *USA Today* report is that there are half a million teenagers on juice these days, almost half of whom, according to a University of Kentucky study, are so naive they think that steroids *without exercise* will build muscle. In this second stone age, the America of Schwarzkopf and Schwarzenegger, someone needs to tell them that bigger isn't necessarily better. Sometimes, bigger is deader.

# *Bruce Lee*

## Terrence Rafferty

*Terrence Rafferty has reviewed films for* The Nation, Sight and Sound, The Atlantic, *and* The New Yorker, *where this piece first appeared.*

Bruce Lee, whatever you think of his art, *was* one of a kind. Most martial-arts pictures are crudely made and grindingly monotonous. When they're enjoyable, it's usually because the stunts are cleverly staged, and have the effect of good slapstick: their ingenuity and their improbability make you laugh. Bruce Lee's fight scenes make you gasp. His moves are fluid and impossibly fast, but there's nothing blurry about them: he snaps off each gesture so decisively, so precisely, that it imprints itself on the mind's eye, and every battle also accommodates moments of exquisitely posed stillness. The rhythm of these scenes is virtuosic, exhilarating. You feel as if you were watching a form of expression that transcends knockabout comedy and macho brawling. (You sort of forget about the star's opponents.) What Bruce Lee does in these set pieces, which constitute the only real value of the crummy-looking and absurdly plotted movies that contain them, is more like inventive choreography superbly executed. James Coburn, who was a student and a friend of Bruce Lee's, called him "the Nijinsky of martial arts," and that's not a ludicrous judgment. Bruce Lee turned aggression into a thing of beauty, a ballet of revenge.

# *Phat, Dude! Huge Air!—*
# *Tony Hawk*

## John M. Glionna

*John M. Glionna is a staff writer for the* Los Angeles Times, *from which this piece is taken.*

Tony Hawk's roller-coaster flight of speed and grace begins here, atop a yawning rickety-looking pile of plywood and bolts at an Encinitas skate park.

His board balanced by feet more nimble than many people's hands, he contemplates a takeoff from the precipice of the 11-foot-high, U-shaped track called a half-pipe. Then Hawk soars. Silently, with a slight kick of the board, he floats for one breathless moment, airborne for a freeze-framed nanosecond, before descending into the depths of lacquered track.

Barnstorming up the other side, Hawk launches his body 10 feet into the air above the lip—twisting, turning, seemingly reckless as he reaches between his legs to take hold of the board. Then, without so much as a flinch, it's back down across the concave half-pipe, soaring past the brim for another of the patented 100 trick moves he has invented or improved since he began skateboarding as a 9-year-old in San Diego, 20 years ago.

At six-foot-three and 170 pounds, the flying Hawk is all elbows and armpits, his spine arching at angles extreme enough to make your back ache just watching him, his frame resembling some modern-day Ichabod Crane, a gangly Big Bird in midflight.

Immediately come the awestruck reviews: "Ohhhhhhh," gasp two dozen or so gawking onlookers.

"That was phat, man," says a freckled 12-year-old. "Huge air!"

"Damn, the guy just doesn't fall."

"Oh my God, what was that?"

"An ollie-tailgrab-to-fakie, stupid. Don't you know?"

To the hard-core believers—these 10-year-old boys with kneepads and helmets and bare-chested teens with bandannas and schoolyard smirks—Tony Hawk is the undisputed skateboard heavyweight of the world, the master-blaster of this strangely subversive sport—a hybrid of street surfing, gymnastics, and balls-out vertical skating. Hawk is the King: Michael Jordan on a 32-by-9-inch hunk of hardwood. Air Tony.

Kids hyperventilate when they meet him. Because, dude, the Hawk man rarely, if ever, falls. And not just that. He started skating when he was a rug rat, just like them, a kid who Just Said No to organized sports such as baseball, forsaking those bossy coaches and pansy uniforms for the individual freedoms of his rebel skateboard.

But here's the really weird part: Parents like Tony Hawk, too. People over 30, who've never been on a skateboard their entire lives, have watched his aerial antics on ESPN's X Games.

What they see is a performer who, at age 29, is closer to their age than that of their children, not some slouching teenage slacker with a "Go to Hell" attitude carving up curbs and benches with a board. Hawk is just like them, a husband and father and a real-life businessman—a partner in Birdhouse Projects, a leading manufacturer of skateboards and accessories.

Hawk endures his sport's juvenile-delinquent fringe element. At skating events, he remains a loner who punches his clock on

110

the half-pipe, staying clear of skateboarding's unleashed partying atmosphere. Away from the skate park, he remains a regular guy who never turns down a request for an autograph, a skater who's maintained the innocent demeanor of some Got Milk? ad amid the antics of those teenage suburban anarchists boasting stomach tattoos and pierced lower lips.

He's a soft-spoken professional, driven by the standards set by his late father, who was among organized skateboarding's earliest promoters. Hawk keeps skating because he still sees room for improvement. There are moves he hasn't mastered, tricks that, quite frankly, still scare him. It's a grown man's work ethic that draws him back to this world dominated by the young and the restless.

Still, something about watching Hawk transcends sports: You don't have to be a skater to marvel at his command of his board, just as you don't have to understand basketball to appreciate a soaring Jordan.

But it's the young skaters—the skinny kids in their formative, pre-confidence years—who are most drawn to Hawk. They know that his wimpy arms and stickman frame drove Hawk to devise a smarter way to fly, one that uses his entire body to propel the board. They know that he has worked on tricks for weeks at a time, taking fall after bloody fall, finally able to do things with a board that older skaters at first mocked but that, years later, admitted are, well, just cerebral.

At 14, Hawk became the youngest professional skateboarder ever, and he has gone on to win scores of vertical events, more than anyone in the sport's history. At 17, he bought his first home. Meanwhile, Hawk has endured countless bangs and bruises that might have sidelined lesser competitors: knee surgery, broken teeth and ribs, concussions, and dozens of sprained wrists and blue-black ankles.

Kids love that stuff.

Tony attributes much of his high flight to the other supportive Hawks, a poster family for the southern California lifestyle.

There's sister Pat, a former backup singer for Michael Bolton and the Righteous Brothers; brother Steve, an accomplished surfer and editor of *Surfer* magazine; sister Lenore, a bilingual education coordinator for the Solana Beach school system; and mother Nancy, a stay-at-home mom who earned a bachelor's degree in her 50s and has since added two master's degrees and a doctorate.

Most important, there was Frank, his sometimes overbearing father, who created two different leagues so his son could have an arena to compete in, allowing Tony to skate nearly unscathed through several dips in his sport's popularity. In the span of a decade, Tony Hawk careened from a $200,000 annual salary in the 1980s to having to borrow money from his wife for his favorite Taco Bell fast-food fix in the drought years of the early 1990s.

Now, resisting impulses to quit in order to spend more time with his four-year-old son, Riley, Hawk remains poised to ride the crest of what could be skateboarding's biggest surge, ready to assume his role as this counterculture sport's bridge to the mainstream.

Already he's performed in 25 skating videos and has had bit parts in several films. He's done commercials for Campbell's soup, Levi's, Gatorade, Coca-Cola, Mountain Dew, Gillette razors, and AT&T, and he once skated as Tony the Tiger in a Frosted Flakes commercial.

Hawk recently finished a 30-stop national tour before jetting off for exhibitions throughout Japan and Switzerland, competing for first-place money that can reach $10,000. In between, he's posing for magazine shoots, meeting with directors for a possible HBO movie, and helping design his company's new computer Web site.

But Hawk is also the old man of skateboarding, an aging gunslinger all the upstarts are aching to call into the street. Slowly, in whispers at tour events, professionals 10 years his junior are questioning Hawk's courage to risk something new.

Not these kids at the Encinitas skate park, though. They watch spellbound as Hawk sails high for another daredevil aerial.

Then it happens: Hawk loses his balance. Collapsing, he uses his kneepads to slide to an abrupt halt on the half-pipe floor. The crowd gasps. For a lingering moment, Hawk-the-Hero stays crouched in a huddled ball, his helmet resting on his knees.

For one lingering moment, Tony Hawk is human.

To big Frank Hawk, that lovable lug of a father with the bad heart, the news that day in 1979 came like an angina attack. His youngest son, Tony, was quitting Little League baseball to pursue a sport that didn't have teams or coaches or that all-out-hustle attitude. The 11-year-old wanted to pursue skateboarding.

Years earlier, Steve Hawk had given his younger brother his first board, a Bahne fiberglass model, and showed him a few tricks. After that first ride outside his house in Tierrasanta, a San Diego suburb, when he yelled to Steve, "Hey, how do I turn this thing?" Tony was hooked.

"Every time I went to the skate park, I would leave thinking I was better than when I came," he reflects. "I never felt that way with baseball. And skateboarding was such an individual thing. If you messed up, you didn't let the team down."

But Frank was to become the local Little League president the next year. For many fathers, this would have been a declaration of war, a perfect time to trot out the old "not as long as you're living in my house" speech.

Not Frank. The decorated navy pilot, who flew during World War II and in Korea, didn't play that game. In his life, he worked halfheartedly at various sales jobs—from musical equipment to used cars—taking every opportunity to rush home to his kids.

Pat Hawk recalls her dad as a rough-edged individualist: "He was just this side of Archie Bunker—thank God he was a Democrat. He didn't have a lot of friends. I just imagine people thinking, 'Oh, God, here comes Frank Hawk again.' With my dad, his kids were his friends."

Whatever the kids wanted was O.K. with Frank. When Pat wanted to become a rock singer, he drove her to lessons and gigs, even built her a P.A. system. When Steve took to surfing, Frank chauffeured him to the beach.

It was no different with Tony. Soon, Frank, too, quit baseball and began driving Tony and his friends to local skate parks. In 1980, Frank organized the California Amateur Skateboard League (CASL). For other skateboarders, though, competing in a league just wasn't cool—especially one started by somebody's father.

Tony bore the brunt of the tension. With every contest he won came the unspoken hint among other skaters that this was Frank Hawk's show, so his son just had to win. "It was hard for me to do my own thing, with the way my dad got so involved," Tony recalls. "But now I see he was the guy who stepped in and got organized skateboarding started when no one else would. Looking back, I don't understand how he could have been working. He must not have been, with all the hours he spent at the skate park."

Frank relished his role as family cabdriver, taking Tony and his friends to meets and practice, always stopping for a wholesome meal, Frank-style: Bob's Big Boy, baked potatoes with the works, In-N-Out specials.

Still, while Tony's parents welcomed visiting skaters to Hotel Hawk for some nurturing atmosphere, there remained an unspoken rift between father and son.

When Frank was just being Frank, barking at kids in his rough-hewn Montana accent for cutting in front of his son's practice runs at local parks, Tony slipped away in frustration. At competitions, he wouldn't even make eye contact with his father. "I always tried to distance myself from him, but he knew what was going on," Tony says. "Maybe he was hurt, I don't know. Once he told me, 'If you don't want me so involved, you can get your own ride to the skate park.'" The strain intensified after Frank, in 1983, created the professional National Skateboard Association, working like an unpaid beast of burden to organize national events that his son usually won.

Détente finally came the following year, the afternoon Frank thought he was having his third heart attack. He and Tony were home alone, and as they waited for the ambulance, Tony told his father how much he loved him, how he was the greatest dad, how much he appreciated everything he had done. Those sentiments fueled Frank like nothing before. As Tony grew older, when he bought his own homes, Frank was there, barging through the front door with his toolbox, building porches and skate ramps in the backyard.

Until March 1995.

That's when Frank found out he wasn't going to die of a bad heart after all. The diagnosis was inoperable lung cancer. By July, Frank's health had plummeted. Tony was preparing for an out-of-town event and his father insisted he not stick around to baby-sit the old man.

From the road, Tony called to say "I love you, Dad," but Frank wouldn't be drawn into a maudlin scene. "I know you do," Frank whispered into the telephone. "But you still can't have my Bud Light."

More than 250 people attended Frank Hawk's funeral. There were eulogies published in skateboard magazines and one written by son Steve in *Surfer* magazine.

The family spread most of Frank's ashes in the ocean off San Diego, but Tony has one last plan to memorialize his father. In a drawer at home, he has kept a Baggie with some of the ashes. One day soon, he will go to the Home Depot in Oceanside, Frank's second home. There he will spread the remaining ashes on the scuffed-up floor.

Explains Tony: "I think my dad would get a kick out of that."

This is what becomes of a young boy's dream to become the best skateboarder on the planet:

On a blazing-hot, late-summer afternoon, Tony Hawk stands in the back parking lot of an Ontario outlet mall, being interviewed by a mini-skirted radio personality who probably wouldn't know an ollie (the basic move of popping the board into the air with your feet) from a Wilson (slipping on a board like a banana peel, named after Mr. Wilson of the Dennis the Menace cartoon series.)

He answers her questions with a few shy, mostly monosyllabic responses that show how much more graceful Hawk is riding a skateboard than he is talking about it. Later, he'll skate-crash through a banner to open a new virtual-reality video arcade inside the mall.

The stunt preceded a six-week tour during which Hawk and several other professional skaters, sponsored by his Birdhouse Projects company, traveled by Winnebago to cities from Overland Park, Kansas, and Kalamazoo, Michigan, to Beltsville, Maryland.

At the Ontario mall, Hawk looks uncomfortable with the attention, just as he did during this year's X Games in San Diego when ESPN announcers fawned over his every move. Hawk had asked them to give more airtime to other skaters, but they assured him more viewers would be attracted to the relatively unknown sport if they concentrated on its star.

"People say I'm the Michael Jordan of skateboarding, but to me, that's all just X Games hype," Tony says. "I'm no Michael Jordan. I've just always had the desire to keep getting better, no matter what standard I've reached. Maybe people read that intensity as greatness. For me, it's just finding something new to do with a skateboard."

When he turned professional in the early '80s, skaters dismissed Hawk's gawky style as mere circus moves. Those were pro skateboarding's infancy days, before the modern-day half-pipe, when skaters blasted about the bowls and over the concrete lips of empty swimming pools. Skateboarding magazines wouldn't interview him. Riders laughed behind his back.

"But what Hawk was showing them all was the future of skateboarding," says Stacy Peralta, Hawk's former sponsor. "Tony had achieved a way to launch a board out of the pool with the sheer force of his body, to achieve incredible heights."

Then came the 1986 movie that would forever change skateboarding. And Tony Hawk's life. *The Search for Animal Chin* was one of a series of documentary-style skateboarding films directed by Peralta and featuring kids such as Tony doing incredible new tricks with their boards in a new $55,000 phenomenon known as the double half-pipe, which Peralta had built in Oceanside.

It was the *Hard Day's Night* of skate films, and young Tony was its mop-headed star. After taking their boards to the streets when pool skating died years before, kids around the country started building their own ramps. The films launched the popularity of the Bones Brigade, the team of skaters, including Hawk, assembled by sponsor Powell Peralta, at the time a leading manufacturer of skateboard equipment and apparel.

Vertical riding was back. And throughout the rest of the 1980s, the Bones Brigade became the Chicago Bulls of skateboarding, hogging the top spots at nearly every contest.

Those were heady days for Hawk. A new Tony Hawk signature skateboard marketed by Powell Peralta sold 20,000 in one month, and Tony got one dollar for every board sold. In 1986, at age 17, he paid $124,000 for a house in Carlsbad and later added one in rural Fallbrook.

Still, the doubters remained.

As Steve Hawk recalls: "In 1986, after *Sports Illustrated* did a story on Tony, there were letters to the magazine for weeks from people saying, 'How could you devote six pages to a skateboarder? That's not a sport!'"

Through it all, Tony stayed close to his roots. When he wasn't touring as part of the Bones Brigade, he was at home playing computer games with friends, driving his venerable, beat-up old Honda Civic.

There were pressures, though. Judges began to grade him more critically; every run had to be perfect. By the late 1980s, Hawk considered quitting competitive skateboarding. "I had done it so long and had reached the level I had wanted to reach," he says. "It wasn't fun anymore."

And in the fickle, topsy-turvy world of vertical skateboarding, the popularity of which rises and falls like a skater on a half-pipe, strange things were happening: A meaner, harder edge to advertising and promotion was introduced by a cadre of smaller skateboard-accessory companies aiming for a piece of the financial pie.

The image of skateboarder as street punk intensified—antisocial little mall rats riding boards pasted with skulls and crossbones. During that same time, first Stacy Peralta and then Hawk left Powell Peralta, and the number of sponsored contests plummeted.

For the first time in Hawk's life, money became an issue. His then-wife, Cindy, a manicurist, gave him a few dollars every week for food and gas—money his friends starting calling the Taco Bell allowance.

It was in the belly of those days that Hawk hooked up with Per Welinder, a Swedish skater with business sense, who had an idea that the two could start their own skateboard company. They could market their products using the strength of their assembled team of skaters, not through shock advertising (such as an ad one company ran in a skateboard magazine, showing 40 ways to kill yourself).

So Tony sold the Fallbrook house and took a second mortgage on the one in Carlsbad—all to raise his half of the $100,000 needed for a start-up investment. "It was a roll of the dice," he says. "Here was everything I'd worked for all my life, and I was willing to drop it all into one last stab at things."

They started the Huntington Beach–based Birdhouse Projects in 1992, and the company has become a leading skateboard and accessory manufacturer—due partly to a line of Tony Hawk signature skateboards, shirts, and stickers. Last year, Birdhouse grossed more than $14 million, up from $800,000 just two years before.

And thanks to exposure from events such as the X Games, vertical skateboarding is back on top once again, this time with a newer, younger generation of skaters, all anxious to take a swipe at Hawk. Most readily admit he is still the best. But at some events, there are rumblings: Hawk is getting too old to keep pace with the new skating styles. Just maybe, they say, the Hawk should retire.

"Most guys are doing new stuff, but Tony sticks to the tricks he did years ago," says 21-year-old Australian skater Tas Pappas, who has bested Hawk at several events. "Most people think Tony Hawk is some kind of god, but not everyone. Know what I mean?"

Standing in the garage of his new home in Carlsbad, Tony-Hawk-the-dad points to the miniature quarter-pipe he built, Frank-like, for his son, Riley. "He could do an ollie at, like, three years old," Tony says proudly.

Nowadays, Hawk also has a new lease on his personal life. Too much time on the road helped end his first marriage, he says. He has joint custody of Riley, and Tony and his second wife, Erin—a former professional in-line skater—have talked about a child or two of their own.

Meanwhile, father and son are inseparable. When Hawk is not touring, he drives Riley to swim class to watch him paddle around. Most afternoons, there's Tony, sitting poolside, using his cellular phone while Riley chugs back and forth in the public pool.

Tony would love to see Riley pick up the skateboard but doesn't push him. Encouragement is the key. Let the boy take his own direction.

Just like Frank.

Friends and family say Tony has rarely sought the skateboarding spotlight, so it will be no shock when he finally drops his board for golf clubs. His gift to the sport will always be his fierce longevity, and there are a million other ways Hawk can contribute.

Like working to change skateboarding's bad-boy image, the stigma existing even in his hometown of Carlsbad, where it is banned in many public places. Hawk could be the perfect diplomat to drive home the point that, as the bumper stickers say, SKATEBOARDING IS NOT A CRIME.

"People see surfers as rebels," he says, "but in a positive way—and skateboarders as the bad rebels. What they don't realize is that the kids wouldn't be in their face so much—out there on the street, carving up curbs and park benches—if they'd just provide them someplace to skate."

These days, Hawk divides his time equally between skateboarding events and his duties at Birdhouse, which include organizing promotions and supervising the company's dozen sponsored skaters. That's not about to change anytime soon.

"I've already been through one surge of popularity in the sport, and I know it doesn't last forever," he says, his voice understated, almost shy. "It's tough, having a family and all, but I've got to skate while the skating is good.

"I have a feeling that I'll know when it's time to hang it up. It'll just come to me."

Still, he is torn. While his greatest fear is fading out, becoming the athlete who stuck around a season too long, something drives him toward the road at the mention of another tour or competitive event.

Leaving for the most recent U.S. tour, he hugged a weeping Erin and said that he wouldn't be doing it much longer, that this might well be his last long trip.

"But," as she noted later, "there's always that qualifier in there."

# *Secretariat*

## William Nack

*William Nack is a senior writer for* Sports Illustrated *and the author of* Secretariat: The Making of a Champion, *from which this piece is taken.*

I threw myself with a passion into that final week before the Belmont. Out to the barn every morning, home late at night, I became almost manic. The night before the race, I called Laurin at home and we talked for a long while about the horse and the Belmont. I kept wondering, What is Secretariat going to do for an encore? Laurin said, "I think he's going to win by more than he has ever won in his life. I think he'll win by ten."

I slept at the *Newsday* offices that night, and at 2 A.M. I drove to Belmont Park to begin my vigil at the barn. I circled around to the back of the shed, lay down against a tree, and fell asleep. I awoke to the crowing of a cock and watched as the stable workers showed up. At 6:07, Hoeffner strode into the shed, looked at Secretariat, and called out to Sweat, "Get the big horse ready! Let's walk him about fifteen minutes."

Sweat slipped into the stall, put the lead shank on Secretariat and handed it to Davis, who led the colt to the outdoor walking ring. In a small stable not thirty feet away, pony girl Robin Edelstein knocked a water bucket against the wall. Secretariat, normally a docile colt on a shank, rose up on his hind legs, pawing at the sky, and started walking in circles. Davis cowered below, as if beneath a thunderclap, snatching at the chain and begging the horse to come down. Secretariat floated back to earth. He danced around the ring as if on springs, his nostrils flared and snorting, his eyes rimmed in white.

Unaware of the scene she was causing, Edelstein rattled the bucket again, and Secretariat spun in a circle, bucked and leaped in the air, kicking and spraying cinders along the walls of the pony barn. In a panic, Davis tugged at the shank, and the horse went up again, higher and higher, and Davis bent back yelling, "Come on down! Come on down!"

I stood in awe. I had never seen a horse so fit. The Derby and Preakness had wound him as tight as a watch, and he seemed about to burst out of his coat. I had no idea what to expect that day in the Belmont, with him going a mile and a half, but I sensed we would see more of him than we had ever seen before.

Secretariat ran flat into legend, started running right out of the gate and never stopped, ran poor Sham into defeat around the first turn and down the backstretch and sprinted clear, opening two lengths, four, then five. He dashed to the three-quarter pole in 1:09⅕, the fastest six-furlong clocking in Belmont history. I dropped my head and cursed Turcotte: *What is he thinking about? Has he lost his mind?* The colt raced into the far turn, opening seven lengths past the half-mile pole. The timer flashed his astonishing mile mark: 1:34⅕!

I was seeing it but not believing it. Secretariat was still sprinting. The four horses behind him disappeared. He opened ten. Then twelve. Halfway around the turn, he was fourteen in front . . . fifteen . . . sixteen . . . seventeen. Belmont Park began to shake. The whole place was on its feet. Turning for home, Secretariat was twenty in front, having run the mile and a quarter in 1:59 flat, faster than his Derby time.

He came home alone. He opened his lead to twenty-five . . . twenty-six . . . twenty-seven . . . twenty-eight. As rhythmic as a rocking horse, he never missed a beat. I remember seeing Turcotte look over to the timer, and I looked over too. It was blinking 2:19, 2:20. The record was 2:26⅖. Turcotte scrubbed on the colt, opening thirty lengths, finally thirty-one. The clock flashed crazily: 2:22 . . . 2:23. The place was one long, deafening roar. The colt seemed to dive for the finish, snipping it clean at 2:24.

I bolted up the press box stairs with exultant shouts and there yielded a part of myself to that horse forever.

# The Greatest Game of H-O-R-S-E in History

## From *The Golden Boys*

## Cameron Stauth

**M**agic and Michael walked past, on their way to the floor. Jordan had the hint of a Wilt-style mustache and goatee. He said the goatee symbolized vacation. A year earlier, no one could have guessed that the Olympics would be a vacation. But the world had changed. The two other primary basketball powers—the Soviet Union and Yugoslavia—had ceased to exist. It had been a tumultuous year, both in world politics and in the lives of the American players.

When Magic and Michael got to the floor, Magic started tossing in his "junior skyhook," the move he'd learned from Kareem that looks easy—until you try to do it. Magic ran the baseline left to right, leaped off his left foot, and feathered in the ball with his right hand. "Nobody can do that," Magic said, grinning at Michael. His face glowed.

"Let's see," said Jordan. He swept across the lane, leaped, lofted it. *Swish.*

"Lu-u-u-ck," said Magic. "Do it again."

He did it again. When the ball fell out of the net, it made a soft echo pop on the floor of the empty stadium.

"Okay, smart aleck," said Magic, "do this." He walked a few steps away from the hoop, palmed the ball, and hooked it under his leg toward the basket. It rattled in. The Magic smile.

Drexler and Pippen were shooting on the other side of the floor. They started watching. Jordan made the under-the-leg shot. "My turn," Jordan said. He walked to the sidelines and stood out of bounds. Eyed the hoop. Pushed it up. *Swish.*

"That's a Mike Smrek shot!" boomed Magic, invoking the name of a notably bad shooter.

"M. J.!" Pippen yelled, signaling for the ball.

"Let Magic make that one first," Jordan said, his little mustache wrinkling into a smile.

Magic shot; missed. "Okay, here's the deal," said Magic. "You got to keep callin' the shot 'til you miss, and you can't shoot the same shot twice." He looked at Pippen. "You wanna play?"

"Sure!"

"You in?" Magic asked Clyde. Drexler beamed and nodded. Drexler knew how good he was, but he wasn't sure everyone else knew.

"Okay, I'll start," said Magic.

"Uh-uh!" cried Jordan." You just missed."

"Good!" said Magic. "Everybody agrees." Magic stepped back to take his shot. Nobody bitched. He was, after all, Magic. He'd been the king of the playground since he was ten years old. Besides, he had even greater authority now. He was fighting the most serious battle of all of them. He might well lose that battle. But the way he was fighting—smiling, acting . . . like Magic—was majestic, and it had elevated him even farther.

Magic looked at the basket—but tossed the ball to Pippen.

Pippen dribbled twice, paused. He planted his feet, crouched, faced the basket, and tossed the ball between his legs—into the hoop. Then Magic made it. Everybody else missed. Pippen's ball again. He stood at the top of the key, held the ball over his head with both hands, and hurled it at the floor. It bounced up and in.

"Ohhh!" said Jordan. "I've seen him do that."

"Then you oughta be able to do it," said Magic. Off to the side, Chris Mullin stood watching, a ball tucked under his arm.

With a jerk of his head, Magic signaled Mullin to join the game.

Jordan tried Pippen's bounce shot. Made it. Magic poked his fist into the air. "Nice!" Then it was his turn, though, and he missed. So did Drexler and Mullin.

"I got one that's not in anybody's repertoire," said Magic. He took the ball just past the free-throw line and dribbled in for what looked like a layup. But he sailed under the glass, then shot from behind the backboard. The ball floated high into the air, hit the front of the rim, and plunked in. The other players roared. Jordan doubled over, holding his belly. Magic's face looked like it was going to explode with happiness.

"I've got one," Clyde said softly. Clyde looked beatific, as if being included in this game meant more to him than any All-Star Game he'd ever played.

"Let's see it," said Jordan.

Clyde walked to the top of the key, angled off to one side, paused, then knifed toward the hoop. He leaped into the air, reaching a height that usually only Jordan hit, but moving forward with even more horizontal force than Jordan. It was his famous glide. As he neared the basket, he pushed the ball toward the hoop. Pulled it back. Glided more. Jerked it toward the hoop again. Smashed it down.

"Ohhh, shit," said Mullin, turning away.

"Oh, no, you don't!" shouted Magic, tossing the ball to Mullin. "You're up." Mullin did a pale, awkward imitation of it. What could he do? He had white man's disease: He couldn't jump. But Magic, Pippen, and Jordan made it.

There wasn't a sound in the stadium except for the cries of the players. It was still virtually empty. Over the past year, as I'd traveled from city to city to spend time with each Olympian, this was what so many of them had talked about as their idea of heaven: an empty gym, with just a few of the best players on earth. No fans. No money. No pressure. No broadcasters. No score. Just . . . a game.

So much is made of the player's work ethic. More important than that is his play ethic. Excellence doesn't come from drudgery. It comes from love.

Magic grabbed the ball and walked to the free-throw line. He faced away from the basket, squared his shoulders, and flipped the ball backward, over his head. *Rip!*

None of these shots had been perfected during college or pro practices, nor certainly during games. They were playground shots. They were the shots of children—not powerful multimillionaires.

"Still my ball," said Magic, after most of the guys had missed his backward shot. He stood on his left foot and lifted his right leg high into the air, like a drunken stork. Then he canted his head at a bizarre angle and fired up the shot. *Rip!*

Nobody else made it. Magic looked ecstatic. The past week had been like a narcotic to him, filling him with the irresistible temptation to come out of retirement. To do so might shorten his life. But for him, basketball *was* his life.

Mullin grabbed the ball and hit from outside the three-point line. The other players all made his shot. But then—to get around the rules of not shooting the same shot twice—he just moved a few feet to the side and shot again. Perfect. But they all made it. He moved again—perfect. This time, they didn't all make it.

"Bor—r-r-ring!" Jordan moaned.

"How 'bout this, then?" Mullin said, marching back to the half-court line. He sized up the basket and heaved the ball. The shot took a hard rattle around the rim and went down. "Still bored?" said Mullin.

"I am," said Magic. He walked to the half-court and swished it. But nobody else made it.

"Watch," said Clyde. He pitched the ball from straight in front of the hoop, well behind the three-point line. It hit the glass and banked in. Only great shooters know how hard that shot is.

"*Jeeze!*" Magic yelped. "That's a Mike Brown shot," he yelled, referring to the clumsy Utah shooter.

Magic glanced at the courtside seats. They were beginning to fill with spectators, all of them slack-jawed at stumbling upon the greatest game of H-O-R-S-E in basketball history.

There will probably never again be a playground game quite like this, because it was unlikely that so extraordinary a team would ever again be assembled. This week NBA Commissioner David Stern had said the next Olympic team would probably be about half college and half pro. Stern hated all of the bitching about "overkill." He was in the midst of an unprecedented expansion of the NBA to the rest of the world, and the last thing he needed was for his boys to look like vicious bullies. Besides, it had become clear this week that the U.S. team with only a few pros could kick ass against any team on the globe.

So this was a once-in-a-lifetime event.

"You want to see a real three-pointer?" Jordan said to Clyde. "Observe." Jordan grabbed the ball with his left hand on top and pushed up a left-hander. It rattled in.

"Owww!" said Magic.

"Nothin' personal, guys!" said Jordan, strutting around in a little one-man parade. "I don't mean to rub it in."

Magic lined up his left-handed three. It clanged off. Again, Magic looked at the spectators out of the corner of his eye. They seemed to make him uneasy. This was a part of him that wasn't meant for the public. It was too precious for that.

"Let's wrap it up, guys," he said. "You talkin' about threes? I'll show you a three." He stood just behind the line. Studied the basket. Closed his eyes. Squeezed them tight to show: Look, no cheating. With one soft, liquid motion, he arced it toward the rim. *Swish!*

"Whoa!" Magic exulted. "I still got it."

The others tried, but no one came close. Simple reason. It's impossible.

"I won!" Magic crowed.

"Who says?" Jordan said.

"I made the last one. And I made the most. You're just gonna have to live with it."

Clyde and Michael laughed and gave each other a high-five.

# The Last Man in the Marathon

## Bud Greenspan

*Bud Greenspan is considered the official chronicler of the Olympic Games. This selection is taken from his* 100 Greatest Moments in Olympic History.

The marathon run at the 1968 Mexico City Olympics was filled with drama. The legendary Abebe Bikila, who had won the previous two marathons in Rome and Tokyo, was attempting to make it three successive victories. It would add a new dimension to a record he already held, for Bikila at that time was the only marathon runner to ever win that event twice.

Bikila looked strong and was among the leaders at seventeen kilometers, more than one-third into the race. . . . Then suddenly and inexplicably, except to his coach, Negusse Roba, he stepped off the roadway and retired from the race. Roba later told a stunned press conference audience that Bikila had been suffering from a bone fracture in his left leg for several weeks.

Bikila's teammate, Mamo Wolde, knew of the injury and when Bikila left the race, Wolde ran as if he was Bikila's mirror image and was able to give Ethiopia its third successive marathon victory, which he later dedicated to his idol, Abebe.

But the drama of this particular marathon would not end when Wolde crossed the finish line. A little more than an hour later with just a few thousand spectators left in the stands, whistles, motorcycle sounds, and flashing red and green lights gave a macabre effect to the cold, dark Mexico City evening. . . . The word was passed to the press box and filtered to the few thousand faithful spectators who remained in the stadium.

"It's the last runner in the marathon," said one reporter as he stopped typing his story to watch the event developing in front of him.

Into the stadium came John Stephen Akhwari of Tanzania. His leg was bloody and bandaged. Wincing with pain at every step, he pressed on and the thousands, a few minutes before in silence, began a slow, steady clapping.

Akhwari made his painful way around the track and the cheering grew louder. The trek around the track seemed interminable. But finally he hobbled across the finish and the crowd roared as if he had been the winner.

In the press box one columnist was writing this lead to his story.

"Today we have seen a young African runner who symbolizes the finest in the human spirit . . . a performance that gives true meaning to sport . . . a performance that lifts sport out of the category of grown men playing at games . . . a performance that gives meaning to the word courage . . . all honor to John Stephen Akhwari of Tanzania."

Afterward Akhwari was asked why he endured the pain and why, since there was no chance of winning, he did not retire from the race. Akhwari appeared perplexed at the question. Then he simply said, "I don't think you understand. My country did not send me to Mexico City to start the race. They sent me to finish the race."

# Olympic Kayaking 2000

## Steve Rushin

*Steve Rushin is a senior writer for* Sports Illustrated.

If you've never sat in 90-degree heat, eating a Crumbed Cutlet of Prawn, on the outskirts of Emu Plains, beside a man-made river, to watch a Frenchman paddle a canoe, you'll be forgiven for thinking it's no spectator sport. Certainly, none of the celebrity fans omnipresent in Olympic Park—Chelsea Clinton, Bill Gates, Rupert Murdoch—crossed the khaki-colored plains west of Sydney to see the slalom finals of canoe and women's kayak. But then the Clintons don't much care for whitewater, which was everywhere in evidence on the $3.6-million, wood-and-concrete, raging river that human chutzpah created in the parched municipality of Penrith, home of Whitewater Stadium, an amusement-park flume ride on growth hormones.

The 320-meter "river" was really a malevolent Maytag machine, into which canoeists (men only) and kayakers (men and women) voluntarily dumped themselves, like dirty linens, into the spin cycle. Paddlers must get from start to finish as fast as possible without touching any of the 23 slalom gates along the way. This is, of

135

course, an unreasonable request, made all the more so by the six gates athletes must navigate while paddling upstream, against a current of 14 cubic meters of water per second. It's the rough equivalent of going over Niagara Falls in a barrel, then dog-paddling back up it again.

Yet far and away the most contentious force encountered by paddlers in Penrith was the public address announcer, a man whose voice needed no electronic amplification, a man who kept shouting, "If you don't dig this mess, you've got the wrong address!" Having evidently apprenticed at monster-truck rallies, he did play-by-play over the loudspeaker, as they do in bad baseball movies: "He's just carving up this course . . . ooh, there's a pretty upstream . . . beautiful river-feel by this paddler. . . ." We novices, paddle-addled, attempted to keep up.

There were 12,500 of us, standing room only, pounding down prawn sandwiches as paddlers went off every two and a half minutes to the kind of ear-piercing techno music favored by German disc jockeys. It all seemed unnecessary in the Walden-like world of carbon-fiber conveyances, but then this is a television age, and some 30 television cameras, many of them remote controlled and mobile, kept a Cyclopsean eye trained on every inch of the course.

To further capture the feel of mass-marketed American spectator extravaganzas, organizers nicknamed the most perilous parts of the white-water run: Vortex, Knuckles, Twilight Zone, Funnel Web, and Deep Fryer. Earlier in the week a photographer had slipped and fallen into one of these diabolical rapids, holding his camera aloft, like a periscope, as he went under the water. This set up an excellent joke. Q: Are there any fish in this river? A: There is one snapper. But the photographer was, alas, rescued.

Chances are he was there to shoot Tony Estanguet, the number-one-ranked 22-year-old from Pau, France, who is on his way to becoming—and here's an image to exercise the imagination— the Michael Jordan of canoeing. Estanguet represented his nation in

Sydney after eliminating his brother Patrice in French qualifying. "I knew he was the obstacle to my dream," says Estanguet, who found few other obstacles in these finals: The combined time of his two runs, each of which lasted less than two minutes, was nearly two seconds faster than that of the silver medalist. In a sport often measured in hundredths of a second (or $\frac{1}{25}$ of an eye blink), a two-second victory is Secretariat-like. Or as the P.A. announcer put it about this paddling prodigy: "Everyone else is just playing volleyball."

The women's kayak final, which came afterward, was won by 32-year-old Stepanka Hilgertova, the 1996 gold medalist and reigning world champion. Hilgertova hails from the Czech Republic, where canoeing and kayaking enjoy immense popularity.

Not only is kayak the only palindromic sport in the Olympics, but it's a palindromic piece of equipment as well, bow and stern largely indistinguishable. Is the sport coming or going? By day's end, the answer was clear: Coming, to judge by the reaction of spectators, who felt unexpectedly forlorn when the racing was over, and the medals awarded, and we found ourselves up this artificial creek, suddenly without a paddle.

# A. J. and the Volcano

## Jim Murray

*Jim Murray was honored by the National Sportscasters and Sportswriters Association as Sportswriter of the Year a record fourteen times. This selection was taken from his book* The Great Ones.

The thing about Anthony Joseph, or A. J., Foyt, is, you might call him "the terrible-tempered Mr. Foyt"—but first, his disposition would have to improve 100 percent before his temper could merely be called "terrible." Calling what Foyt does "terrible" is like calling the sinking of the *Titanic* "unfortunate."

Foyt wasn't born mad, but he made up for it.

People just seem to get on his nerves. He wins the pole in the temper derby by 20 miles an hour. If they named a car after him it would be called the Volcano.

Some guys run on methanol. A. J. runs on rage. He drives as if he were sorry there are no pedestrians.

A. J. plays no favorites. He bullies the car, the track, his own pit crew, mechanic, the stewards, starters, press, and public with equal fervor. Anyone who would go down to A. J.'s pit at race time would go into a lion cage at feeding time.

A. J. just wants the world to keep off his rear wheels. He doesn't want society tailgating on him. If he can see you in his rearview mirror, you're too damn close. He's as irritable on race day as a guy whose pants are too tight. When he won at Indy on closed-circuit TV one year, they shoved a glass of milk in his mouth, and A. J. sprayed it all over the ground and made a face that would have soured the milk.

He doesn't fraternize with the other drivers. "I don't trust nobody," he grumbles. He likes a nice distance between him and his competition, on and off the track.

When asked when he was going to retire, A. J. growled, "When I do, I'll just drive in and park it and say 'To hell with all of you.'" He once ran half a mile from a parked car to punch in the mouth a rival driver whom he thought had shut him off.

He considers himself a better mechanic than anyone he could hire, and the arguments in the Foyt garage frequently drown out the carburetion tests. He has run through more mechanics than Zsa Zsa Gabor has husbands. "Either A. J. or the engine is snarling," his crewmen say.

He bristles when someone suggests the car is more important than the driver in his sport. "It's just a dumb piece of iron," shoots back A. J. "Do you give credit to the baseball when somebody hits a home run? Do you cheer the racket in tennis? A bad driver cannot win even in a good car. But a good driver cannot win in junk."

To be sure, he does not get in junk. A. J. spends more time around the garage than a drop light. "He's either in a car—or under it," his crew admits. There are times when they wish he'd take up polo.

Still, he just may be the world's greatest race driver. It's for sure he's America's. At an age (39) when most of us are afraid to get in our nice, big, two-toned and two-ton Continentals and venture on the freeway, A. J. is still taking on the kids in those open-cockpit, 200-

plus mph, winged speedway brutes and sliding through the corners so high and low in the groove the customers can't bear to look.

When A. J. started racing, engines were in front, you could have all the fuel you could carry or store, and cars were cars and didn't need wings to hold them on track. It was wheel-to-wheel, not clock-to-clock, driving, and there were no flameproof suits or plastic face masks.

The first Indianapolis race he was in, 12 of the 33 drivers in it have since died in a race car, including one, Pat O'Conor, who was to die that day (1958). Of the others, A. J. is the only one still racing. Jimmy Reece, Jud Larson, Al Keller, Short Templeman, Eddie Sachs, Johnny Thomson, Ed Elisian, Jerry Unser, and Art Bish all died on or because of the track.

Mad Anthony is on the pole at Ontario in the California 500 today. He's been on dozens of poles. He's won three Indys and more championship points than any driver alive. He won't announce his retirement, he says, because "four or more of my friends who said they were going to run one more race or two more races died in those races."

Death is always on the pole in this game. No 500-mile guarantee comes with these cars. Neither car nor driver has a warranty.

It could happen to A. J. as it did to so many of the company he started out with. He has walked away from cars on fire and on a stump of an ankle. He has been lifted out of stocks with his back broken.

It's unthinkable to A. J. he would go to join that ghostly company from the starting grid of the 1958 race. But if he does, I'll tell you one thing: God's going to get an awful earful.

# Rodeo Roping

## Red Smith

*Red Smith is considered by this editor the finest sports stylist of the twentieth century. This selection is taken from* Strawberries in the Wintertime.

The thermometer registered 100 degrees when the calf roping started, and spectators were clustered in the shade of live oaks on the slopes that form three sides of a natural amphitheater in Woodlake, California. The first calf came tearing out of the chute with Bob Wiley riding hard at his heels, lariat whistling overhead. In a single unbroken flow of movement, Wiley threw his loop and pitched the slack, came out of the saddle on a dead run, flipped the calf, tied three legs, and flung both hands aloft for the timer. From chute to finish, the operation consumed 10.6 seconds.

Bob Wiley is a lawman, sheriff of Tulare County, and crowds these days aren't much disposed to cheer for the fuzz, but this crowd roared. The flat farmlands of the San Joaquin Valley are sports country—when there's a big high school football game or a major track meet, shopkeepers lock up at noon—and Tulare County's buffs have known Wiley virtually all his 35 years, as the comrade and teammate of Rafer Johnson from the fourth grade through high school, then as a rodeo hand who once ran second to the incomparable Dean Oliver for the world roping championship, and since 1965 as a dedicated officer whose efforts to combat juvenile delinquency have been applauded in the *Congressional Record*.

Wiley is an athlete by nature, a roper by avocation, and a cop by popular demand. Hard campaigning got him his job the first time but when he ran for reelection he swept 78.5 percent of the vote.

When he and Rafe Johnson were on the football and track teams at Kingsburg High, Bob carried 210 pounds on a figure measuring six feet one inch from top to bottom and a trifle less across the shoulders. Now there's an additional 25 pounds under the belt buckle. He walks with the purposeful lurch of a boar grizzly in the mating season and his habitual expression is just this side of a scowl, though on the rare occasions when he smiles it is sudden sunrise. If you drew a seine through Central Casting you couldn't match more exactly the stereotype of a western sheriff.

Wiley was born in Kingsburg, down Highway 99 a piece from Fresno. Rafer Johnson was nine when his family moved in from Hillsboro, Texas, and games soon brought the boys together. In football Rafer was the outside runner and pass receiver. Bob was the other halfback, a straight-ahead smasher and a sensational blocker. Exceptionally fast for his size—he ran 100 yards in 9.9 as a freshman—Bob was leadoff runner and Rafer the anchorman on a relay team that was the talk of the state.

Rafer went to the University of California, Los Angeles, took the silver medal in the decathlon in the 1956 Olympics and four years later won that punishing event in Rome. Bob stayed in San Joaquin Valley and attended Porterville Junior College. He had one of his better days against Reedley Junior College when he gained 279 yards. This got him mention for Little All-America but by that time roping had become an addiction.

The rodeo bug had sunk its fangs in him when he watched a roping in Tulare during his senior year in high school. He paid $50 for an old nag that he hauled in a 17-year-old Chevvy pickup that could make 35 miles an hour downhill when the wind was right. He couldn't travel far, but any weekend when there was a rodeo within driving distance of the campus, he made it.

In 1956 he met Dean Oliver, who had won the world championship once and would win it six times more. Struck by Wiley's speed, strength, and reflexes, Oliver coached the young man, hauled him and mounted him on his own horse. At a few rodeos he even paid Wiley's entrance fees in exchange for one-quarter of his winnings, and The Rope doesn't bet long shots.

From 1960 through 1965 Wiley's average winnings were slightly more than $12,000 a year with a top of $18,180 in 1963, the year he ran second to Oliver. Meanwhile he was working three to five days a week as a deputy in Tulare County. When friends talked him into running for sheriff, his campaign fund was a rope.

In one respect he is a political freak even for California, where oddballs abound: He keeps campaign promises. As a deputy it had bugged him that he seldom got to meet kids unless they were in trouble, so he made the main plank in his platform a pledge to work with the young. Once elected, he heckled his Board of Supervisors for funds to launch the programs.

Now Tulare County deputies seek out youth. Two deputies on special assignment travel from schoolyard to campus to gathering place in a van showing movies and slides or just rapping with the kids. Wiley himself made 97 appearances last year. Figures show a decline in "juvenile related incidents."

Wiley's operation is not exactly like Matt Dillon's. He sits in an up-to-date office in Visalia receiving teletype reports from all over the county's 4,970 square miles. To run a check on a stolen car, he presses a button on a computer. He has a force of 183 in Visalia and three substations. As it was in his college days, rodeo is strictly a weekend proposition now, but as he demonstrated recently in Woodlake he can still go to a calf like an irate mongoose homing in on a cobra.

His friend Rafer Johnson is still in the area. Since the Olympics, Rafer has been a movie actor and a sportscaster; he stumped for Robert F. Kennedy and was present the night of the assassination; now he is with Continental Telephone Corporation as vice-president for personnel. This guy was president of the student body in grammar school, high school, and college, and for the opening of the 1960 Olympics the American team chose him as the leader to carry the flag.

"Sometimes," Wiley says, "I feel I've always been in the shadow of a great guy, Rafer or Dean. Then I think, well, if I'm second, I picked two winners to run behind."

# *The Troubles*

## Tom Chiarella

*Tom Chiarella regularly writes about golf for* Esquire.

I'm driving the Ring of Kerry with three guys named Sullivan. Just of four of us, on this notoriously winding mountain road in southwest Ireland, fresh off an eight-hour Aer Lingus flight, two hours in our shitty Euro-rental Renault pressed in cheek by jowl one against the other, heading to our first stop—like every stop for this next week, a golf course—the Ring of Kerry Golf Club. It's raining. Nasty, cold, sideways-blowing rain. No weather for golf, none whatsoever. More like weather for chess. Weather for fireplaces. Weather for television and pretzels. Wipers slapping this way then that, nary a word passes among us as we careen along the ridgelines, plunge down the slick and narrow mountain roads. At one point, we come to a clutch of driveways where the road is full of massive cows being herded toward a milk shed, forcing us to a dead stop. It is a cliché in the making, four golfers held steady against the ancient commerce of the herdsman. The third Sullivan, who is driving today, takes out his camera just as the road starts to clear, snapping a picture through the windshield.

"Why don't you roll down the window?" the first Sullivan says. "That picture won't come out."

The third Sullivan inches the car forward. "We have a tee time," he says. "We need to get there so we can hit some balls first." In front of us, a border collie bites hard on the leg of a large white cow.

On a sustained Irish golf trip, moments of rest are spent thumbing through tourist brochures for a sense of where the nearest driving range might be. You wake up only to drive to the next course, ninety minutes or more along the hedgerows, between and around the tiny lorries with their loads of tin, their crates of eggs. You play with three guys you know only sort of glancingly from your little club. At the end of the day—wet, mud spattered, blistered, wind-burned, and dry mouthed—you return to distant B&Bs, where you eat your meals and recount the shots and drink your drinks, only to sleep, then rise to do it again.

Don't mistake this for anything but what it is—hard-core golf, not tourism. It is a kind of training, an indulgent discipline, wrought on golf courses as confounding as they are elegant. This is the sort of trip sure to sicken the traveler who dog-ears guidebooks. No museums. No boat rides. No tours of cathedrals. Day after day, the sun rises, the television news drones on, traffic trudges this way and that, and you play golf. Each day is like the last, except in matters of tee-box alignment and crosswinds and depth of heather. There is scenery, to be sure—slate-gray sea, vast deserted beaches, hoary sand dunes sun-baked and spiked with grass. Irish golf courses are beautiful in the same manner that farms are beautiful; there is a sense of care evident, but every aspect of their appearance and practice represents labor. Hard labor, too—not for the greenskeeper so much as for the golfer. Playing them doesn't require calculation so much as commitment.

If you want to get better, to finally raise your game to the next level, find ten days in your life, locate three golfers, fly to Ireland, set the stakes, and play. You will get your butt kicked by something—

the courses, the weather, the grass, the wind. These moments will force you to pull yourself together, to face up to it when a course is just beating you over and over again. Do not stop. Do not quit.

At Waterville, the brutal links course at the very end of County Kerry's Iverngh Peninsula, we set out at 7 A.M. in a driving rain. The holes throb with heather, and the ocean hisses like a big, indifferent ghoul in the distance. The three Sullivans and I stand at the clubhouse, pawing through our bags for earmuffs and plastic bag covers like women rooting in their purses for tampons. Then we head out, straight into the heart of it. At the end of the ninth hole, we find a statue wrapped completely in garbage bags. I point to the giant man, covered in flapping plastic, as we limp in for a cup of tea at the turn.

"What do you think that's about?"

"It's raining," the first Sullivan says. "I bet it's supposed to be a raincoat."

"They're garbage bags," the second Sullivan replies.

The first Sullivan reasserts himself. "I'm telling you, they want you to wear a raincoat. They're telling you to wear a coat. That's the Irish way. They are very considerate."

At this point, it has been raining for thirty-six hours without cease; the other Sullivans won't have it. They don't want to hear theories. They point to the first Sullivan's ball, resting near a puddle at the base of a sand dune.

"What do you lie?" they ask him. The wind picks up. The garbage bags flap in the wind. The next days, on the way to Ballybunion, we read in the paper that the as-yet-to-be-unveiled statue is a likeness of Payne Stewart, the honorary captain at Waterville. "You see?" says the first Sullivan. "I told you they were considerate."

At Ballybunion, we play the new course, a Robert Trent Jones nightmare, into the teeth of a wind that pours off the ocean, cold and foul. The course is all carry, all test and trial, and the caddie master assigns us two bony junior caddies who, instead of watching our shots, shield their eyes against the needlepoints of rain from the shore. I'm determined to get off to a good start, but by the third hole, I'm 9 over par and thinking about walking off. There is soup at the bar, and there are newspapers there and a telephone booth where I can go to call my family. But the third Sullivan is in worse shape than I, having taken a 10 on the first hole, and the course is about to take a sudden, notable lurch toward the sea.

Off the fourth tee, I hit a solid 3-wood, which jump-slides into the heather about 220 yards out. In the deep grass, it takes me a full five minutes to find the ball, which I mark by leaving a hat next to it before turning back to get a club. The Sullivans stand at various points, in the fairway and off, lining up shots. When I return to the grass, I cannot find the hat. The clouds seem to have dropped down on top of us now. I check my line, look for a landmark, and start in again. No luck. While the two caddies help me, the Sullivans hit away. We descend the small hill, poke around in the grass until I am soaked to midthigh. The hat, and the ball next to it, are absolutely gone into the texture of the rolls of tall grass and sand. Having lost a ball, a hat, and the hole in one moment, I cannot make myself walk back to the tee, so I concede the hole and drop a ball. I bear down, punch a 4-iron, and two-putt for an ersatz double bogey. Not all that bad, when you consider the first Sullivan takes a 7, losing two shots in the heather, the second Sullivan cards a par, and the third Sullivan picks up after overshooting the green.

I begin to see this as the essential lesson of Ireland: You are alone with your troubles. Later, when I tell this to the bartender at our hotel, he nods. "An Irish plays through all kind of shit. An Irish plays on."

One day, near Killarney, we run into some fair weather, a mere twenty-mile-an-hour wind, the sunshine glorious though intermittent. That day, we're off the links courses, away from the ocean, at the Killeen Course at Killarney Golf and Fishing Club. My caddie is a hard little guy named Bobby who doesn't want to hear that links golf is harder than the parkland version. "It's the same love grass," he tells me.

"Love grass?"

He points to the heather lining the secondary rough; it's nasty and innocent all at once, like the hair in your armpit. "The tall stuff," he says. "That's the love grass."

I'll bite. "Why do you call it love grass?"

He chomps down on his toothpick. "You go in there," he says, "and you're fucked for sure."

Today the sun shines. It has been five days of struggle, my best moments unwitnessed, my putting troubles tossed like dice around the dinner table. When I land in a trap at seventeen—the deepest trap, Bobby says, in all of Ireland—Bobby shakes his head.

"Tom," he says, "you have to tell yourself one thing."

I take the sand wedge from him and start up the fairway. "What's that?"

"There are tougher shots than the one you have to hit," he says. "You have to convince yourself that you are up to it."

I'm five days in. I have seen all manner of trouble. I am beginning to get golf muscles. The trap is probably twelve feet deep with a sheer face, hugging the green. It takes the first Sullivan seven shots to get out, and even then he has to hit it out into the fairway to do it. My ball has slid back into a flat lie. My rounds used to collapse around moments such as this. I climb into the trap, place my weight on my left foot, open my club face absurdly far, and swing hard. The ball rises and settles fifteen feet from the pin. Simple. In a matter of moments, I will three-putt.

Bobby gives me a hand out of the trap. One of the Sullivans murmurs something, but no one says much. It doesn't matter. It's just another tough shot. Bobby's right. There's a tougher shot somewhere in Ireland. I'm likely to see it tomorrow, or the next day, or on the next hole. I'm beginning to understand I'm up to it.

# *The XFL*

## Bill Plaschke

*Bill Plaschke writes a sports column for the* Los Angeles Times, *from which this piece is taken.*

With about six minutes left in the first quarter Saturday, the Xtreme's Tommy Maddox scored the first touchdown by a Los Angeles pro football team in the Coliseum in more than six years.

I missed it.

I was talking to Cindy, Shanna, and Roberta.

They were sitting in a section behind the end zone.

Only, it wasn't a Dawg Pound or Black Hole sort of section.

It was a hot tub sort of section.

Wearing bikinis the size of sweatbands, beers in their hands, water up to their necks, the three women had just completed the most impressive drive of this game.

Earlier Saturday afternoon, someone affiliated with the Xtreme had phoned their place of employment, the Spearmint Rhino gentleman's club.

"Get us three strippers down here, and fast," the official reportedly said.

The three women—Cindy says she is a waitress—piled into a car and drove to the Coliseum.

Once there, amid 45-degree temperatures, they climbed gingerly into a hot tub filled with rubber duckies and proceeded to wave for the camera, gyrate for the crowd, splish and splash. Three quarters later, they were still there.

I'm not really sure what happened in the football game. In the words of the wrestling people who run this new XFL league, I don't know who was whupped, whomped, wasted, or whiplashed.

But I do know who was wrinkled.

The game was good enough to write about.

If only the XFL made it that easy.

If only this could be about a local team of NFL castoffs mounting a fourth-quarter comeback in its home debut to win a game in double overtime.

But the Xtreme's 39–32 victory over the Chicago Enforcers Saturday in the second week of the inaugural XFL season?

A sidebar.

The main story begins with how there was just as much action among the 35,813 in the Coliseum stands, with bottles being thrown, breasts being bared, and one fight that nearly knocked the loser into the visiting bench.

"It ain't fair," said one official working the Enforcers sideline. "These guys talk trash to the fans, and then when the bottles fly, they are protected with pads. I don't have any pads."

Pat Lynch, Coliseum general manager, issued this statement through a spokesman:

"It was no more rowdy than a USC game."

I guess I missed that USC game when one fan, apparently off his rocker, stood with his arms raised and absorbed a horrific five-minute pelting of popcorn and beer and trash.

I guess I also missed that USC game when the entire side of the Coliseum turned and chanted at a young woman to pull up her shirt, wildly applauding when she did.

"I'm very concerned," said J. K. McKay, the Xtreme general manager. "I don't know exactly what we will do, but something will be done. We will fix this. People cannot cross the line."

That line Saturday wasn't just crossed with fists. It was also crossed with taste.

This sort of chaos is a common occurrence in professional wrestling, the first passion of XFL founder Vince McMahon. It's just a little unsettling to see it with its arms around a sport that's supposed to be real. There was a cursing pregame welcome from that wrestler known as The Rock. There were dirty-dancing cheerleaders on strip-joint-style stages.

And don't forget our friends in the hot tub. "I think it's a little bit hokey, to tell you the truth," said Shanna.

She calls it hokey. I call it, males ages 18–34.

That is the demographic that this new league is trying to attract. I know, because The Rock told me so. He actually used that word, "demographic."

"Those are the kind of people we are obviously trying to reach," The Rock said after announcing to the screaming crowd that the NFL should stick it where the sun doesn't shine. "We are looking for people who want entertainment, who want to have a good time."

Statistics have proved that playing to this audience sells. A stroll through countless black shirts and scowls Saturday showed that anyone else is pretty much not welcome.

"Hey, seven rows up, a pretty girl," said Bob Muldowney, the mobile camera driver underneath the NBC sideline camera.

"You looking for pretty girls?" I asked.

"You going to point them out to me?" he said.

Muldowney asked if I was writing a story about the game. "Yes," I said.

"In the sports section?" he asked.

"Good question," I replied.

The shame of Saturday was that through all the gadgetry and wires and running cameramen and enough equipment to make it look like a movie set, there were a couple of good football performances. Somebody named Jeremaine Copeland caught 190 yards' worth of passes for the Xtreme, many of them while leaping over two defenders. Old friend Tommy Maddox scrambled and ducked and threw for 388 yards and four touchdown. But even with all that, there was lingering odor. As with anything touched by Vince McMahon, you have to wonder. Was it real?

Did the Xtreme, after being totally outclassed for three quarters, really rebound to score twice in the final three minutes of regulation? Were the Enforcers suddenly that easy to shut out in the second half after scoring 25 points in the first half?

Watching from the sidelines, with some impossible catches and diving misses, it seemed real. Watching the players in the locker room afterward, their joy unrestrained, it seemed real.

"How could you possibly script that?" McKay asked. "How could you make all those great catches?"

Also considering that Las Vegas has endorsed the sport with regular gambling lines, scripting would seem improbable. As improbable as having a ticket stub that reads, HOT TUB.

# *The Most Dangerous Game*

## Richard Connell

*Richard Connell wrote his most famous short story in 1924. His novels include* Murder at Sea *and* What Ho! *He died in 1949.*

Off there to the right—somewhere—is a large island," said Whitney. "It's rather a mystery—"

"What island is it?" Rainsford asked.

"The old charts call it 'Ship-Trap Island,'" Whitney replied. "A suggestive name, isn't it? Sailors have a curious dread of the place. I don't know why. Some superstition—"

"Can't see it," remarked Rainsford, trying to peer through the dank tropical night that was palpable as it pressed its thick warm blackness in upon the yacht.

"You've good eyes," said Whitney, with a laugh, "and I've seen you pick off a moose moving in the brown fall bush at four hundred yards, but even you can't see four miles or so through a moonless Caribbean night."

"Nor four yards," admitted Rainsford. "Ugh! It's like moist black velvet."

"It will be light in Rio," promised Whitney. "We should make it in a few days. I hope the jaguar guns have come from Purdey's. We should have some good hunting up the Amazon. Great sport, hunting."

"The best sport in the world," agreed Rainsford,

"For the hunter," amended Whitney. "Not for the jaguar."

"Don't talk rot, Whitney," said Rainsford. "You're a big-game hunter, not a philosopher. Who cares how a jaguar feels?"

"Perhaps the jaguar does," observed Whitney.

"Bah! They've no understanding."

"Even so, I rather think they understand one thing—fear. The fear of pain and the fear of death."

"Nonsense," laughed Rainsford. "This hot weather is making you soft, Whitney. Be a realist. The world is made up of two classes—the hunters and the huntees. Luckily, you and I are hunters. Do you think we've passed that island yet?"

"I can't tell in the dark. I hope so."

"Why?" asked Rainsford.

"The place has a reputation—a bad one."

"Cannibals?" suggested Rainsford.

"Hardly. Even cannibals wouldn't live in such a God-forsaken place. But it's gotten into sailor lore, somehow. Didn't you notice that the crew's nerves seemed a bit jumpy to-day?"

"They were a bit strange, now you mention it. Even Captain Nielsen—"

"Yes, even that tough-minded old Swede, who'd go up to the devil himself and ask him for a light. Those fishy blue eyes held a look I never saw there before. All I could get out of him was: 'This place has an evil name among sea-faring men, sir.' Then he said to me, very gravely: 'Don't you feel anything?'—as if the air about us was actually poisonous. Now, you mustn't laugh when I tell you this—I did feel something like a sudden chill.

"There was no breeze. The sea was as flat as a plate-glass window. We were drawing near the island then. What I felt was a—a mental chill; a sort of sudden dread."

"Pure imagination," said Rainsford. "One superstitious sailor can taint the whole ship's company with his fear."

"Maybe. But sometimes I think sailors have an extra sense that tells them when they are in danger. Sometimes I think evil is a tangible thing—with wave lengths, just as sound and light have. An evil place can, so to speak, broadcast vibrations of evil. Anyhow, I'm glad we're getting out of this zone. Well, I think I'll turn in now, Rainsford."

"I'm not sleepy," said Rainsford. "I'm going to smoke another pipe up on the after deck."

"Good night, then, Rainsford. See you at breakfast."

"Right. Good night, Whitney."

There was no sound in the night as Rainsford sat there, but the muffled throb of the engine that drove the yacht swiftly through the darkness, and the swish and ripple of the wash of the propeller.

Rainsford, reclining in a steamer chair, indolently puffed on his favorite brier. The sensuous drowsiness of the night was on him. "It's so dark," he thought, "that I could sleep without closing my eyes; the night would be my eyelids—"

An abrupt sound startled him. Off to the right he heard it, and his ears, expert in such matters, could not be mistaken. Again he heard the sound, and again. Somewhere off in the blackness, some one had fired a gun three times.

Rainsford sprang up and moved quickly to the rail, mystified. He strained his eyes in the direction from which the reports had come, but it was like trying to see through a blanket. He leaped upon the rail and balanced himself there, to get greater elevation; his pipe, striking a rope, was knocked from his mouth. He lunged for it; a short, hoarse cry came from his lips as he realized he had reached too far and had lost his balance. The cry was pinched off short as the blood-warm waters of the Caribbean Sea closed over his head.

He struggled up to the surface and tried to cry out, but the wash from the speeding yacht slapped him in the face and the salt water in his open mouth made him gag and strangle. Desperately he struck out with strong strokes after the receding lights of the yacht, but he stopped before he had swum fifty feet. A certain cool-headedness had come to him; it was not the first time he had been in a tight place. There was a chance that his cries could be heard by some one aboard the yacht, but that chance was slender, and grew more slender as the yacht raced on. He wrestled himself out of his clothes, and shouted with all his power. The lights of the yacht became faint and ever-vanishing fireflies; then they were blotted out entirely by the night.

Rainsford remembered the shots. They had come from the right, and doggedly he swam in that direction, swimming with slow, deliberate strokes, conserving his strength. For a seemingly endless time he fought the sea. He began to count his strokes; he could do possibly a hundred more and then—

Rainsford heard a sound. It came out of the darkness, a high screaming sound, the sound of an animal in an extremity of anguish and terror.

He did not recognize the animal that made the sound; he did not try to; with fresh vitality he swam toward the sound. He heard it again; then it was cut short by another noise, crisp, staccato.

"Pistol shot," muttered Rainsford, swimming on.

Ten minutes of determined effort brought another sound to his ears—the most welcome he had ever heard—the muttering and growling of the sea breaking on a rocky shore. He was almost on the rocks before he saw them; on a night less calm he would have been shattered against them. With his remaining strength he dragged himself from the swirling waters. Jagged crags appeared to jut into the opaqueness; he forced himself upward, hand over hand. Gasping, his hands raw, he reached a flat place at the top. Dense jungle came down to the very edge of the cliffs. What perils that tangle of trees and underbrush might hold for him did not concern Rainsford just then. All he knew was that he was safe from his enemy, the sea, and that utter weariness was on him. He flung himself down at the jungle edge and tumbled headlong into the deepest sleep of his life.

When he opened his eyes he knew from the position of the sun that it was late in the afternoon. Sleep had given him new vigor; a sharp hunger was picking at him. He looked about him, almost cheerfully.

"Where there are pistol shots, there are men. Where there are men, there is food," he thought. But what kind of men, he wondered, in so forbidding a place? An unbroken front of snarled and ragged jungle fringed the shore.

He saw no sign of a trail through the closely knit web of weeds and trees; it was easier to go along the shore, and Rainsford floundered along by the water. Not far from where he had landed, he stopped.

Some wounded thing, by the evidence a large animal, had thrashed about in the underbrush; the jungle weeds were crushed down and the moss was lacerated; one patch of weeds was stained crimson. A small, glittering object not far away caught Rainsford's eye and he picked it up. It was an empty cartridge. "A twenty-two," he remarked. "That's odd. It must have been a fairly large animal too. The hunter had his nerve with him to tackle it with a light gun. It's clear that the brute put up a fight. I suppose the first three shots I heard was when the hunter flushed his quarry and wounded it. The last shot was when he trailed it here and finished it."

He examined the ground closely and found what he had hoped to find—the print of hunting boots. They pointed along the cliff in the direction he had been going. Eagerly he hurried along, now slipping on a rotten log or a loose stone, but making headway; night was beginning to settle down on the island.

Bleak darkness was blacking out the sea and jungle when Rainsford sighted the lights. He came upon them as he turned a crook in the coastline, and his first thought was that he had come upon a village, for there were many lights. But as he forged along he saw to his great astonishment that all the lights were in one enormous building—a lofty structure with pointed towers plunging upward into the gloom. His eyes made out the shadowy outlines of a palatial chateau; it was set on a high bluff, and on three sides of it cliffs dived down to where the sea licked greedy lips in the shadows.

"Mirage," thought Rainsford. But it was no mirage, he found, when he opened the tall spiked iron gate. The stone steps were real enough; the massive door with a leering gargoyle for a knocker was real enough; yet about it all hung an air of unreality.

He lifted the knocker, and it creaked up stiffly, as if it had never before been used. He let it fall, and it startled him with its booming loudness. He thought he heard steps within; the door remained closed. Again Rainsford lifted the heavy knocker, and let it fall. The door opened then, opened as suddenly as if it were on a spring, and Rainsford stood blinking in the river of glaring gold light that poured out. The first thing Rainsford's eyes discerned was the largest man Rainsford had ever seen—a gigantic creature, solidly made and black-bearded to the waist. In his hand the man held a long-barreled revolver, and he was pointing it straight at Rainsford's heart.

Out of the snarl of beard two small eyes regarded Rainsford.

"Don't be alarmed," said Rainsford, with a smile which he hoped was disarming. "I'm no robber. I fell off a yacht. My name is Sanger Rainsford of New York City."

The menacing look in the eyes did not change. The revolver pointed as rigidly as if the giant were a statue. He gave no sign that he understood Rainsford's words, or that he had even heard them. He was dressed in uniform, a black uniform trimmed with gray astrakhan.

"I'm Sanger Rainsford of New York," Rainsford began again. "I fell off a yacht. I am hungry."

The man's only answer was to raise with his thumb the hammer of his revolver. Then Rainsford saw the man's free hand go to his forehead in a military salute, and he saw him click his heels together and stand at attention. Another man was coming down the broad marble steps, an erect, slender man in evening clothes. He advanced to Rainsford and held out his hand.

In a cultivated voice marked by a slight accent that gave it added precision and deliberateness, he said: "It is a very great pleasure and honor to welcome Mr. Sanger Rainsford, the celebrated hunter, to my home."

Automatically Rainsford shook the man's hand.

"I've read your book about hunting snow leopards in Tibet, you see," explained the man. "I am General Zaroff."

Rainsford's first impression was that the man was singularly handsome; his second was that there was an original, almost bizarre quality about the general's face. He was a tall man past middle age, for his hair was a vivid white; but his thick eyebrows and pointed military mustache were as black as the night from which Rainsford had come. His eyes, too, were black and very bright. He had high cheek bones, a sharp-cut nose, a spare, dark face, the face of a man used to giving orders, the face of an aristocrat. Turning to the giant in uniform, the general made a sign. The giant put away his pistol, saluted, withdrew.

"Ivan is an incredibly strong fellow," remarked the general, "but he has the misfortune to be deaf and dumb. A simple fellow, but, I'm afraid, like all his race, a bit of a savage."

"Is he Russian?"

"He is a Cossack," said the general, and his smile showed red lips and pointed teeth. "So am I."

"Come," he said, "we shouldn't be chatting here. We can talk later. Now you want clothes, food, rest. You shall have them. This is a most restful spot."

Ivan had reappeared, and the general spoke to him with lips that moved but gave forth no sound.

"Follow Ivan, if you please, Mr. Rainsford," said the general. "I was about to have my dinner when you came. I'll wait for you. You'll find that my clothes will fit you, I think."

It was to a huge, beam-ceiling bedroom with a canopied bed big enough for six men that Rainsford followed the silent giant. Ivan laid out an evening suit, and Rainsford, as he put it on, noticed that it came from a London tailor who ordinarily cut and sewed for none below the rank of duke.

The dining room to which Ivan conducted him was in many ways remarkable. There was a medieval magnificence about it; it suggested a baronial hall of feudal times with its oaken panels, its high ceiling, its vast refectory table where twoscore men could sit down to eat. About the hall were the mounted heads of many animals—lions, tigers, elephants, moose, bears; larger or more perfect specimens Rainsford had never seen. At the great table the general was sitting, alone.

"You'll have a cocktail, Mr. Rainsford," he suggested. The cocktail was surpassingly good; and, Rainsford noted, the table appointments were of the finest—the linen, the crystal, the silver, the china.

They were eating *borsch,* the rich, red soup with whipped cream so dear to Russian palates. Half apologetically General Zaroff said: "We do our best to preserve the amenities of civilization here. Please forgive any lapses. We are well off the beaten track, you know. Do you think the champagne has suffered from its long ocean trip?"

"Not in the least," declared Rainsford. He was finding the general a most thoughtful and affable host, a true cosmopolite. But there was one small trait of the general's that made Rainsford uncomfortable. Whenever he looked up from his plate he found the general studying him, appraising him narrowly.

"Perhaps," said General Zaroff, "you were surprised that I recognized your name. You see, I read all books on hunting published in English, French, and Russian. I have but one passion in my life, Mr. Rainsford, and it is the hunt."

"You have some wonderful heads here," said Rainsford as he ate a particularly well cooked filet mignon. "That Cape buffalo is the largest I ever saw."

"Oh, that fellow. Yes, he was a monster."

"Did he charge you?"

"Hurled me against a tree," said the general. "Fractured my skull. But I got the brute."

"I've always thought," said Rainsford, "that the Cape buffalo is the most dangerous of all big game."

For a moment the general did not reply; he was smiling his curios red-lipped smile. Then he said slowly: "No. You are wrong, sir. The Cape buffalo is not the most dangerous big game." He sipped his wine. "Here in my preserve on this island," he said in the same slow tone, "I hunt more dangerous game."

Rainsford expressed his surprise. "Is there big game on this island?"

The general nodded. "The biggest."

"Really?"

"Oh, it isn't here naturally, of course. I have to stock the island."

"What have you imported, general?" Rainsford asked. "Tigers?"

The general smiled. "No," he said. "Hunting tigers ceased to interest me some years ago. I exhausted their possibilities, you see. No thrill left in tigers, no real danger. I live for danger, Mr. Rainsford."

The general took from his pocket a gold cigarette case and offered his guest a long black cigarette with a silver tip; it was perfumed and gave off a smell like incense.

"We will have some capital hunting, you and I," said the general. "I shall be most glad to have your society."

"But what game—" began Rainsford.

"I'll tell you," said the general. "You will be amused, I know. I think I may say, in all modesty, that I have done a rare thing. I have invented a new sensation. May I pour you another glass of port, Mr. Rainsford?"

"Thank you, general."

The general filled both glasses, and said: "God makes some men poets. Some He makes kings, some beggars. Me He made a hunter. My hand was made for the trigger, my father said. He was a very rich man with a quarter of a million acres in the Crimea, and he was an ardent sportsman. When I was only five years old he gave me a little gun, specially made in Moscow for me, to shoot sparrows with. When I shot some of his prize turkeys with it, he did not punish me; he complimented me on my marksmanship. I killed my first bear in the Caucasus when I was ten. My whole life has been one prolonged hunt. I went into the army—it was expected of noblemen's sons—and for a time commanded a division of Cossack cavalry, but my real interest was always the hunt. I have hunted every kind of game in every land. It would be impossible for me to tell you how many animals I have killed."

The general puffed at his cigarette.

"After the debacle in Russia I left the country, for it was imprudent for an officer of the Czar to stay there. Many noble Russians lost everything. I, luckily, had invested heavily in American securities, so I shall never have to open a tea room in Monte Carlo or drive a taxi in Paris. Naturally, I continued to hunt—grizzlies in your Rockies, crocodiles in the Ganges, rhinoceroses in East Africa. It was in Africa that the Cape buffalo hit me and laid me up for six months. As soon as I recovered I started for the Amazon to hunt jaguars, for I had heard they were unusually cunning. They weren't." The Cossack sighed. "They were no match at all for a hunter with his wits about him, and a high-powered rifle. I was bitterly disappointed. I was lying in my tent with a splitting headache one night when a terrible thought pushed its way into my mind. Hunting was beginning to bore me! And hunting, remember, had been my life. I have heard that in America business men often go to pieces when they give up the business that has been their life."

"Yes, that's so," said Rainsford.

The general smiled. "I had no wish to go to pieces." he said. "I must do something. Now, mine is an analytical mind, Mr. Rainsford. Doubtless that is why I enjoy the problems of the chase."

"No doubt, General Zaroff."

"So," continued the general, "I asked myself why the hunt no longer fascinated me. You are much younger than I am, Mr. Rainsford, and have not hunted as much, but you perhaps can guess the answer."

"What was it?"

"Simply this: hunting had ceased to be what you call 'a sporting proposition.' It had become too easy. I always got my quarry. Always. There is no greater bore than perfection."

The general lit a fresh cigarette.

"No animal had a chance with me any more. That is no boast; it is a mathematical certainty. The animal had nothing but his legs and his instinct. Instinct is no match for reason. When I thought of this it was a tragic moment for me, I can tell you."

Rainsford leaned across the table, absorbed in what his host was saying.

"It came to me as an inspiration what I must do," the general went on.

"And that was?"

The general smiled the quiet smile of one who has faced an obstacle and surmounted it with success. "I had to invent a new animal to hunt," he said.

"A new animal? You're joking."

"Not at all," said the general. "I never joke about hunting. I needed a new animal. I found one. So I bought this island, built this house, and here I do my hunting. The island is perfect for my purposes—there are jungles with a maze of trails in them, hills, swamps—"

"But the animal, General Zaroff?"

"Oh," said the general, "it supplies me with the most exciting hunting in the world. No other hunting compares with it for an instant. Every day I hunt, and I never grow bored now, for I have a quarry with which I can match my wits."

Rainsford's bewilderment showed in his face.

"I wanted the ideal animal to hunt," explained the general. "So I said: 'What are the attributes of an ideal quarry?' And the answer was, of course: 'It must have courage, cunning, and, above all, it must be able to reason.'"

"But no animal can reason," objected Rainsford.

"My dear fellow," said the general, "there is one that can."

"But you can't mean—" gasped Rainsford.

"And why not?"

"I can't believe you are serious, General Zaroff. This is a grisly joke."

"Why should I not be serious? I am speaking of hunting."

"Hunting? Good God, General Zaroff, what you speak of is murder."

The general laughed with entire good nature. He regarded Rainsford quizzically. "I refuse to believe that so modern and civilized a young man as you seem to be harbors romantic ideas about the value of human life. Surely your experiences in the war—"

"Did not make me condone cold-blooded murder," finished Rainsford stiffly.

Laughter shook the general. "How extraordinarily droll you are!" he said. "One does not expect nowadays to find a young man of the educated class, even in America, with such a naive, and, if I may say so, mid-Victorian point of view. It's like finding a snuff-box in a limousine. Ah, well, doubtless you had Puritan ancestors. So many Americans appear to have had. I'll wager you'll forget your notions when you go hunting with me. You've a genuine new thrill in store for you, Mr. Rainsford."

"Thank you, I'm a hunter, not a murderer."

"Dear me," said the general, quite unruffled, "again that unpleasant word. But I think I can show you that your scruples are quite ill founded."

"Yes?"

"Life is for the strong, to be lived by the strong, and, if need be, taken by the strong. The weak of the world were put here to give the strong pleasure. I am strong. Why should I not use my gift? If I wish to hunt, why should I not? I hunt the scum of the earth—sailors from tramp ships—lascars, blacks, Chinese, whites, mongrels—a thorobred horse or hound is worth more than a score of them."

"But they are men," said Rainsford hotly.

"Precisely," said the general. "That is why I use them. It gives me pleasure. They can reason, after a fashion. So they are dangerous."

"But where do you get them?"

The general's left eyelid fluttered down in a wink. "This island is called Ship-Trap," he answered. "Sometimes an angry god of the high seas sends them to me. Sometimes, when Providence is not so kind, I help Providence a bit. Come to the window with me."

Rainsford went to the window and looked out toward the sea.

"Watch! Out there!" exclaimed the general, pointing into the night. Rainsford's eyes saw only blackness, and then, as the general pressed a button, far out to sea Rainsford saw the flash of lights.

The general chuckled. "They indicate a channel," he said, "where there's none: giant rocks with razor edges crouch like a sea monster with wide-open jaws. They can crush a ship as easily as I crush this nut." He dropped a walnut on the hardwood floor and brought his heel grinding down on it. "Oh, yes," he said, casually, as if in answer to a question, "I have electricity. We try to be civilized here."

"Civilized? And you shoot down men?"

A trace of anger was in the general's black eyes, but it was there for but a second, and he said, in his most pleasant manner: "Dear me, what a righteous young man you are! I assure you I do not do the thing you suggest. That would be barbarous. I treat these visitors with every consideration. They get plenty of good food and exercise. They get into splendid physical condition. You shall see for yourself to-morrow."

"What do you mean?"

"We'll visit my training school," smiled the general. "It's in the cellar. I have about a dozen pupils down there now. They're from the Spanish bark *San Lucar* that had the bad luck to go on the rocks out there. A very inferior lot, I regret to say. Poor specimens and more accustomed to the deck than to the jungle."

He raised his hand, and Ivan, who served as waiter, brought thick Turkish coffee. Rainsford, with an effort, held his tongue in check.

"It's a game, you see," pursued the general blandly. "I suggest to one of them that we go hunting. I give him a supply of food and an excellent hunting knife. I give him three hours' start. I am to follow, armed only with a pistol of the smallest caliber and range. If my quarry eludes me for three whole days, he wins the game. If I find him"—the general smiled—"he loses."

"Suppose he refuses to be hunted?"

"Oh," said the general, "I give him his option, of course. He need not play that game if he doesn't wish to. If he does not wish to hunt, I turn him over to Ivan. Ivan once had the honor of serving as official knouter to the Great White Czar, and he has his own ideas of sport. Invariably, Mr. Rainsford, invariably they choose the hunt."

"And if they win?"

The smile on the general's face widened. "To date I have not lost," he said.

Then he added, hastily: "I don't wish you to think me a braggart, Mr. Rainsford. Many of them afford only the most elementary sort of problem. Occasionally I strike a tartar. One almost did win. I eventually had to use the dogs."

"The dogs?"

"This way, please. I'll show you."

The general steered Rainsford to a window. The lights from the windows sent a flickering illumination that made grotesque patterns on the courtyard below, and Rainsford could see moving about there a dozen or so huge black shapes; as they turned toward him, their eyes glittered greenly.

"A rather good lot, I think," observed the general. "They are let out at seven every night. If anyone should try to get into my house—or out of it—something extremely regrettable would occur to him." He hummed a snatch of song from the Folies Bergère.

"And now," said the general, "I want to show you my new collection of heads. Will you come with me to the library?"

"I hope," said Rainsford, "that you will excuse me to-night, General Zaroff. I'm really not feeling at all well."

"Ah, indeed?" the general inquired solicitously. "Well, I suppose that's only natural, after your long swim. You need a good, restful night's sleep. To-morrow you'll feel like a new man, I'll wager. Then we'll hunt, eh? I've one rather promising prospect—"

Rainsford was hurrying from the room.

"Sorry you can't go with me tonight," called the general. "I expect rather fair sport—a big, strong black. He looks resourceful—Well, good night, Mr. Rainsford; I hope you have a good night's rest."

The bed was good, and the pajamas of the softest silk, and he was tired in every fiber of his being, but nevertheless Rainsford could not quiet his brain with the opiate of sleep. He lay, eyes wide open. Once he thought he heard stealthy steps in the corridor outside his room. He sought to throw open the door; it would not open. He went to the window and looked out. His room was high up in one of the towers. The lights of the chateau were out now, and it was dark and silent, but there was a fragment of sallow moon, and by its wan light he could see, dimly, the courtyard; there, weaving in and out in the pattern of shadow, were black, noiseless forms; the hounds heard him at the window and looked up, expectantly, with their green eyes. Rainsford went back to the bed and lay down. By many methods he tried to put himself to sleep. He had achieved a doze when, just as morning began to come, he heard, far off in the jungle, the faint report of a pistol.

General Zaroff did not appear until luncheon. He was dressed faultlessly in the tweeds of a country squire. He was solicitous about the state of Rainsford's health.

"As for me," sighed the general, "I do not feel so well. I am worried, Mr. Rainsford. Last night I detected traces of my old complaint."

To Rainsford's questioning glance the general said: "Ennui. Boredom."

Then, taking a second helping of Crepes Suzette, the general explained: "The hunting was not good last night. The fellow lost his head. He made a straight trail that offered no problems at all. That's the trouble with these sailors; they have dull brains to begin with, and they do not know how to get about in the woods. They do excessively stupid and obvious things. It's most annoying. Will you have another glass of Chablis, Mr. Rainsford?"

"General," said Rainsford firmly, "I wish to leave this island at once."

The general raised his thickets of eyebrows; he seemed hurt. "But, my dear fellow," the general protested, "you've only just come. You've had no hunting—"

"I wish to go to-day," said Rainsford. He saw the dead black eyes of the general on him, studying him. General Zaroff's face suddenly brightened.

He filled Rainsford's glass with venerable Chablis from a dusty bottle.

"To-night," said the general, "we will hunt—you and I."

Rainsford shook his head. "No, general," he said. "I will not hunt."

The general shrugged his shoulders and delicately ate a hot-house grape. "As you wish, my friend," he said. "The choice rests entirely with you. But may I not venture to suggest that you will find my idea of sport more diverting than Ivan's?"

He nodded toward the corner to where the giant stood, scowling, his thick arms crossed on his hogshead of chest.

"You don't mean—" cried Rainsford.

"My dear fellow," said the general, "have I not told you I always mean what I say about hunting? This is really an inspiration. I drink to a foeman worthy of my steel—at last."

The general raised his glass, but Rainsford sat staring at him.

"You'll find this game worth playing," the general said enthusiastically. "Your brain against mine. Your woodcraft against mine. Your strength and stamina against mine. Outdoor chess! And the stake is not without value, eh?"

"And if I win—" began Rainsford huskily.

"I'll cheerfully acknowledge myself defeated if I do not find you by midnight of the third day," said General Zaroff. "My sloop will place you on the mainland near a town."

The general read what Rainsford was thinking.

"Oh, you can trust me," said the Cossack. "I will give you my word as a gentleman and a sportsman. Of course you, in turn, must agree to say nothing of your visit here."

"I'll agree to nothing of the kind," said Rainsford.

"Oh," said the general, "in that case—But why discuss that now? Three days hence we can discuss it over a bottle of Veuve Cliquot, unless—"

The general sipped his wine.

Then a businesslike air animated him. "Ivan," he said to Rainsford, "will supply you with hunting clothes, food, a knife. I suggest you wear moccasins; they leave a poorer trail. I suggest too that you avoid the big swamp in the southeast corner of the island. We call it Death Swamp. There's quicksand there. One foolish fellow tried it. The deplorable part of it was that Lazarus followed him. You can imagine my feelings, Mr. Rainsford. I loved Lazarus; he was the finest hound in my pack. Well, I must beg you to excuse me now. I always take a siesta after lunch. You'll hardly have time for a nap, I fear. You'll want to start, no doubt. I shall not follow till dusk. Hunting at night is so much more exciting than by day, don't you think? Au revoir, Mr. Rainsford, au revoir."

General Zaroff, with a deep, courtly bow, strolled from the room. From another door came Ivan. Under one arm he carried khaki hunting clothes, a haversack of food, a leather sheath containing a long-bladed hunting knife; his right hand rested on a cocked revolver thrust in the crimson sash about his waist. . . .

Rainsford had fought his way through the bush for two hours. "I must keep my nerve. I must keep my nerve," he said through tight teeth.

He had not been entirely clear-headed when the chateau gates snapped shut behind him. His whole idea at first was to put distance between himself and General Zaroff, and, to this end, he had plunged along, spurred on by the sharp rowels of something very like panic. Now he had got a grip on himself, had stopped, and was taking stock of himself and the situation.

He saw that straight flight was futile; inevitably it would bring him face to face with the sea. He was in a picture with a frame of water, and his operations, clearly, must take place within that frame.

"I'll give him a trail to follow," muttered Rainsford, and he struck off from the rude paths he had been following into the trackless wilderness. He executed a series of intricate loops; he doubled on his trail again and again, recalling all the lore of the fox hunt, and all the dodges of the fox. Night found him leg-weary, with hands and face lashed by the branches, on a thickly wooded ridge. He knew it would be insane to blunder on through the dark, even if he had the strength. His need for rest was imperative and he thought: "I have played the fox, now I must play the cat of the fable." A big tree with a thick trunk and outspread branches was nearby, and, taking care to leave not the slightest mark, he climbed up into the crotch, and stretching out on one of the broad limbs, after a fashion, rested. Rest brought him new confidence and almost a feeling of security. Even so zealous a hunter as General Zaroff could not trace him there, he told himself; only the devil himself could follow that complicated trail through the jungle after dark. But, perhaps, the general was a devil—

An apprehensive night crawled slowly by like a wounded snake, and sleep did not visit Rainsford, although the silence of a dead world was on the jungle. Toward morning when a dingy gray was varnishing the sky, the cry of some startled bird focused Rainsford's attention in that direction. Something was coming through the bush, coming slowly, carefully, coming by the same winding way Rainsford had come. He flattened himself down on the limb, and through a screen of leaves almost as thick as tapestry, he watched. The thing that was approaching was a man.

It was General Zaroff. He made his way along with his eyes fixed in utmost concentration on the ground before him. He paused, almost beneath the tree, dropped to his knees and studied the ground. Rainsford's impulse was to hurl himself down like a panther, but he saw that the general's right hand held something metallic—a small automatic pistol.

The hunter shook his head several times, as if he were puzzled. Then he straightened up and took from his case one of his black cigarettes; its pungent incense-like smoke floated up to Rainsford's nostrils.

Rainsford held his breath. The general's eyes had left the ground and were traveling inch by inch up the tree. Rainsford froze there, every muscle tensed for a spring. But the sharp eyes of the hunter stopped before they reached the limb where Rainsford lay; a smile spread over his brown face. Very deliberately he blew a smoke ring into the air; then he turned his back on the tree and walked carelessly away, back along the trail he had come. The swish of the underbrush against his hunting boots grew fainter and fainter.

The pent-up air burst hotly from Rainsford's lungs. His first thought made him feel sick and numb. The general could follow a trail through the woods at night; he could follow an extremely difficult trail; he must have uncanny powers; only by the merest chance had the Cossack failed to see his quarry.

Rainsford's second thought was even more terrible. It sent a shudder of cold horror through his whole being. Why had the general smiled? Why had he turned back?

Rainsford did not want to believe what his reason told him was true, but the truth was as evident as the sun that had by now pushed through the morning mists. The general was playing with him! The general was saving him for another day's sport! The Cossack was the cat; he was the mouse. Then it was that Rainsford knew the full meaning of terror.

"I will not lose my nerve. I will not."

He slid down from the tree, and struck off again into the woods. His face was set and he forced the machinery of his mind to function. Three hundred yards from his hiding place he stopped where a huge dead tree leaned precariously on a smaller, living one. Throwing off his sack of food, Rainsford took his knife from its sheath and began to work with all his energy.

The job was finished at last, and he threw himself down behind a fallen log a hundred feet away. He did not have to wait long. The cat was coming again to play with the mouse.

Following the trail with the sureness of a bloodhound, came General Zaroff. Nothing escaped those searching black eyes, no crushed blade of grass, no bent twig, no mark, no matter how faint, in the moss. So intent was the Cossack on his stalking that he was upon the thing Rainsford had made before he saw it. His foot touched the protruding bough that was the trigger. Even as he touched it, the general sensed his danger and leaped back with the agility of an ape. But he was not quite quick enough; the dead tree, delicately adjusted to rest on the cut living one, crashed down and struck the general a glancing blow on the shoulder as it fell; but for his alertness, he must have been smashed beneath it. He staggered, but he did not fall; nor did he drop his revolver. He stood there, rubbing his injured shoulder, and Rainsford, with fear again gripping his heart, heard the general's mocking laugh ring through the jungle.

"Rainsford," called the general, "if you are within sound of my voice, as I suppose you are, let me congratulate you. Not many men know how to make a Malay man-catcher. Luckily, for me, I too have hunted in Malacca. You are proving interesting, Mr. Rainsford. I am going now to have my wound dressed; it's only a slight one. But I shall be back. I shall be back."

When the general, nursing his bruised shoulder, had gone, Rainsford took up his flight again. It was flight now, a desperate, hopeless flight, that carried him on for some hours. Dusk came, then darkness, and still he pressed on. The ground grew softer under his moccasins; the vegetation grew ranker, denser; insects bit him savagely. Then, as he stepped forward, his foot sank into the ooze. He tried to wrench it back, but the muck sucked viciously at his foot as if it were a giant leech. With a violent effort, he tore his foot loose. He knew where he was now. Death Swamp and its quicksand.

His hands were tight closed as if his nerve were something tangible that someone in the darkness was trying to tear from his grip. The softness of the earth had given him an idea. He stepped back from the quicksand a dozen feet or so and, like some huge prehistoric beaver, he began to dig.

Rainsford had dug himself in in France when a second's delay meant death. That had been a placid pastime compared to his digging now. The pit grew deeper; when it was above his shoulders, he climbed out and from some hard saplings cut stakes and sharpened them to a fine point. These stakes he planted in the bottom of the pit with the points sticking up. With flying fingers he wove a rough carpet of weeds and branches and with it he covered the mouth of the pit. Then, wet with sweat and aching with tiredness, he crouched behind the stump of a lightning-charred tree.

He knew his pursuer was coming; he heard the padding sound of feet on the soft earth, and the night breeze brought him the perfume of the general's cigarette. It seemed to Rainsford that the general was coming with unusual swiftness; he was not feeling his way along, foot by foot. Rainsford, crouching there, could not see the general, nor could he see the pit. He lived a year in a minute. Then he felt an impulse to cry aloud with joy, for he heard the sharp crackle of the breaking branches as the cover of the pit gave way; he heard the sharp scream of pain as the pointed stakes found their mark. He leaped up from his place of concealment. Then he cowered back. Three feet from the pit a man was standing, with an electric torch in his hand.

"You've done well, Rainsford," the voice of the general called. "Your Burmese tiger pit has claimed one of my best dogs. Again you score. I think, Mr. Rainsford, I'll see what you can do against my whole pack. I'm going home for a rest now. Thank you for a most amusing evening."

At daybreak Rainsford, lying near the swamp, was awakened by a sound that made him know that he had new things to learn about fear. It was a distant sound, faint and wavering, but he knew it. It was the baying of a pack of hounds.

Rainsford knew he could do one of two things. He could stay where he was and wait. That was suicide. He could flee. That was postponing the inevitable. For a moment he stood there, thinking. An idea that held a wild chance came to him, and, tightening his belt, he headed away from the swamp.

The baying of the hounds drew nearer, then still nearer, nearer, ever nearer. On a ridge Rainsford climbed a tree. Down a watercourse, not a quarter of a mile away, he could see the bush moving. Straining his eyes, he saw the lean figure of General Zaroff; just ahead of him Rainsford made out another figure whose wide shoulders surged through the tall jungle weeds; it was the giant Ivan, and he seemed pulled forward by some unseen force; Rainsford knew that Ivan must be holding the pack in leash.

They would be on him any minute now. His mind worked frantically. He thought of a native trick he had learned in Uganda. He slid down the tree. He caught hold of a springy young sapling and to it he fastened his hunting knife, with the blade pointing down the trail; with a bit of wild grapevine he tied back the sapling. Then he ran for his life. The hounds raised their voices as they hit the fresh scent. Rainsford knew now how an animal at bay feels.

He had to stop to get his breath. The baying of the hounds stopped abruptly, and Rainsford's heart stopped too. They must have reached the knife.

He shinned excitedly up a tree and looked back. His pursuers had stopped. But the hope that was in Rainsford's brain when he climbed died, for he saw in the shallow valley that General Zaroff was still on his feet. But Ivan was not. The knife, driven by the recoil of the springing tree, had not wholly failed.

Rainsford had hardly tumbled to the ground when the pack took up the cry again.

"Nerve, nerve, nerve!" he panted, as he dashed along. A blue gap showed between the trees dead ahead. Ever nearer drew the hounds. Rainsford forced himself on toward that gap. He reached it. It was the shore of the sea. Across a cove he could see the gloomy gray stone of the chateau. Twenty feet below him the sea rumbled and hissed. Rainsford hesitated. He heard the hounds. Then he leaped far out into the sea. . . .

When the general and his pack reached the place by the sea, the Cossack stopped. For some minutes he stood regarding the blue-green expanse of water. He shrugged his shoulders. Then he sat down, took a drink of brandy from a silver flask, lit a perfumed cigarette, and hummed a bit from "Madame Butterfly."

General Zaroff had an exceedingly good dinner in his great paneled dining hall that evening. With it he had a bottle of Pol Roger and half a bottle of Chambertin. Two slight annoyances kept him from perfect enjoyment. One was the thought that it would be difficult to replace Ivan; the other was that his quarry had escaped him; of course the American hadn't played the game—so thought the general as he tasted his after-dinner liqueur. In his library he read, to soothe himself, from the works of Marcus Aurelius. At ten he went up to his bedroom. He was deliciously tired, he said to himself, as he locked himself in. There was a little moonlight, so, before turning on his light, he went to the window and looked down at the courtyard. He could see the great hounds, and he called: "Better luck another time," to them. Then he switched on the light.

A man, who had been hiding in the curtains of the bed, was standing there.

"Rainsford!" screamed the general. "How in God's name did you get here?"

"Swam," said Rainsford. "I found it quicker than walking through the jungle."

The general sucked in his breath and smiled. "I congratulate you," he said. "You have won the game."

Rainsford did not smile. "I am still a beast at bay," he said, in a low, hoarse voice. "Get ready, General Zaroff."

The general made one of his deepest bows. "I see," he said. "Splendid! One of us is to furnish a repast for the hounds. The other will sleep in this very excellent bed. On guard, Rainsford. . . ."

He had never slept in a better bed, Rainsford decided.